The Long Walk

A Pilgrimage from Canterbury to Rome

Robert Muirhead

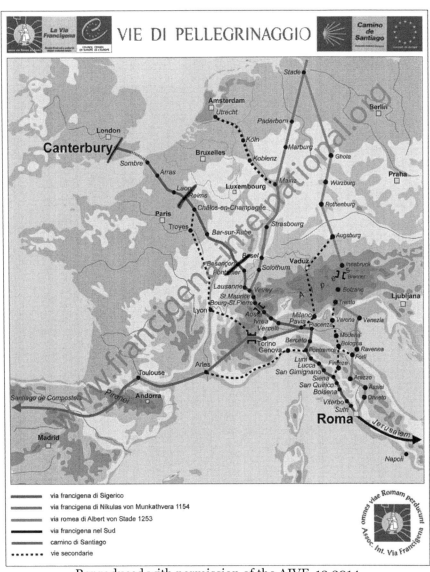

VIE DI PELLEGRINAGGIO

via francigena di Sigerico
via francigena di Nikulas von Munkathvera 1154
via romea di Albert von Stade 1253
via francigena nel Sud
camino di Santiago
vie secondarie

Reproduced with permission of the AIVF, 12.2014

Contents

About the Author

Robert Muirhead travels extensively and has visited more than 120 countries. Photos from his travels have won prizes and have been chosen to illustrate travel websites and other travel publications.

He has made pilgrimages along several of the ancient pilgrimage routes crisscrossing Europe, including the Via Francigena from Canterbury in England to Rome, a distance of over 2,000 kilometres. He has written blogs and articles about these amazing journeys, as well as numerous book reviews for Amazon.

Robert Muirhead was born in Australia and has lived and worked in Hong Kong, Brussels and England. He now lives in Melbourne, Australia.

Other Books by the Author

"Searches—Quests for Meaning."
(www.amazon.com/dp/B00Q67I5ZS).

"A Pilgrim in Europe—How I planned and walked three pilgrimages." (www.amazon.com/dp/B00UMV1SNU).

"Forty Shades of Green—Journeys on the river of life."
(www.amazon.com/dp/B00VZ7K318).

"Journeys in Ancient Lands—Following the Silk Route."
(www.amazon.com/dp/B00XJ43GSW)

Acknowledgments

I must especially thank the Confraternity of Pilgrims to Rome (CPR) for their comprehensive website and accommodation list; and Alison Raju for her guidebook, "The Via Francigena Canterbury to Rome–Parts 1 and 2" (http://www.cicerone.co.uk/author/detail.cfm/author/1283/name/alison-raju). Her guidebook was a great help to me when I was planning the first half of my pilgrimage. William Marques was also very helpful to me when I sought advice on other matters. I hope the few articles I wrote for the CPR newsletter were some return for their help.

I encourage all intending pilgrims to Rome to join the CPR. Here is a link to the CPR website: http://www.pilgrimstorome.org.uk/news.html

Adelaide Trezzini of the Association Internationale Via Francigena (AIVF) generously gave me permission to use one of their maps showing the Via Francigena and other pilgrimage routes linked to it. Here is a link to the AIVF website: http://www.francigena-international.org/newsite/index.php?lang=en

I used Paul Chinn and Babette Gallard's guidebooks during my walk to Rome ("Lightfoot Guide to the Via Francigena", 3 volumes), together with Paul's GPS data. I cannot thank Paul enough for all his help. He responded promptly to all my emails with helpful advice and even emailed new GPS files to me when my GPS unit failed *en route*. I remain indebted to him for all his help and I hope my feedback on his guidebooks has been a partial return of the favour. Here is a link to their website: http://www.pilgrimagepublications.com/aboutpp.html

Writing and updating guidebooks to the Via Francigena is not a path to riches for their authors. It is a niche market, and a lot of ongoing effort is required to keep them up to date. Both Paul Chinn and Alison Raju are doing essential work to bring the Via Francigena alive for increasing numbers of pilgrims and I wish them well for the future. Buy their books!

The Camino de Santiago Forum and its many contributors have been a particularly helpful source of help when planning my walk. Here is a link to the website: https://www.caminodesantiago.me/community/

I stayed for the night at some memorable places and I have tried to give them a special mention in my book. That in no way detracts from the hospitality I received at all the other places which accommodated me for a night. The Via Francigena would be almost impossible without the many dedicated accommodation providers dotted along the route. They are links in a great chain that stretches from Canterbury to Rome.

Introduction

My obsession with the Via Francigena began in St. Jean Pied de Port, France in August 2010. I had just completed the Via Podensis and I was in a pilgrim supply shop chatting with the owner. I said that I had walked the Via Podensis and the Camino de Santiago de Compostela and did not know what to attempt next. He reached under the counter and brought out a guidebook on the Via Francigena. I had never heard of it, but was all ears as he talked about his intention to walk the entire route from Canterbury to Rome in one attempt.

That encounter kindled a hope that one day I might also walk the Via Francigena to Rome. But could I ever complete such a challenging journey? It would be a much greater challenge than any of the other pilgrimage walks I had done.

The more I read, the more daunting it seemed to be. Accommodation was a common problem in accounts of the walk. The route itself could be confusing. Then there is the sheer distance–over 2000 kilometres. I am no longer a downy-faced youth and would be walking alone. Could my aging body stand the rigours of such an arduous journey?

Two years passed while I wrestled with my doubts and found excuses not to begin. But the years pressed in, and the longer I delayed the more difficult it would be.

In the end there was only one way to resolve all doubts, and that was to commence the journey and deal with problems as they arose. Otherwise, I would always wonder what might have been. Too often we take counsel of our fears; when often the difficult way turns out to be the most rewarding of all, if only we have the desire and courage to begin. I decided to compromise by completing the Via Francigena in three long walks over successive years, rather than trying to do the whole walk in one attempt.

Then there was the question of what to take? On previous pilgrimage walks I had carried only a light backpack, water and food. I had found by experience that I had to limit my pack weight to about 7 kilograms if I was to average 25 kilometres per day for the whole walk. It also meant not carrying a tent or camping equipment and being able to find regular accommodation each day. A tent and camping gear would have added an extra few kilograms of weight. Many pilgrims normally carry 12 or 15 kilograms–even more, so camping is a viable option for them.

But difficulties finding accommodation on the Via Francigena might make camping necessary, so I briefly experimented with a towed cart so I could take more gear. There are excellent towed carts available for hikers, but I found them too difficult to use on rough, muddy or steep terrain. Pulling a loaded cart uphill, over obstacles is not easy in practice. Carts are excellent on good flat paths. Nevertheless, I have seen carts used on pilgrimage walks–even an airport-style towed suitcase on one occasion!

In the end, I stuck with my proven pack and a minimalist load list. The pack contained only essentials, such as only one change of clothes, and no luxuries. All extra weight had to be pared back. "If in doubt, throw it out" became my guiding principle when deciding what to take.

About the Via Francigena

The Via Francigena is an ancient road running from France to Rome, but it is usually considered to start in Canterbury, England. The route was known in Italy as the "Via Francigena" (the road from France) or the "Via Romea Francigena" (the road from France to Rome). In medieval times it was an important road and pilgrimage route for those wishing to visit the sacred sites in Rome–or even to continue on to Jerusalem.

There were several possible routes for the Via Francigena which changed over the centuries as trade, the political situation and pilgrimage waxed and waned. Travellers may have used several crossings of the Alps and the Apennines, for example, depending on the season, the popularity of certain shrines and other factors.

About 990 AD, Sigeric the Serious, the new Archbishop of Canterbury, travelled on the Via Francigena to Rome to receive his *pallium* from the Pope. He recorded his route and its 80 stops on the return journey.

A copy of this document was re-discovered in the British Library in the 1980s and has served as the basis of modern efforts to reinvigorate the Via Francigena. Most guidebooks try to follow Sigeric's route, but local walking guides and signposting often direct pilgrims away from busy roads, or to places that may be of interest to local walkers.

In 2004 the Via Francigena was designated a Major Cultural Route by the Council of Europe. This has prompted greater efforts to improve and popularise the Via Francigena to make the journey easier for more than 1200 modern pilgrims who undertake all or part of the journey each year.

About This Book

Writing this book after the Via Francigena posed a new set of problems for me. Such a long walk, occupying about three months over three years, inevitably has high points and low points. There were exhilarating and challenging days, there were routine days; and there were days when I felt demotivated and simply wanted to stay put and rest. Some of the landscape was sublime, but much was not.

I could have simply written about the good experiences and places, and the bad experiences and places. After all, they are what interest readers. But such an account would have been false. Any long pilgrimage is a metaphor for life. There is a beginning and an end. On the way, the pilgrim has hopes and also faces uncertainty and disappointment. The pilgrim's physical condition and health can vary. He or she meets wonderful people, but occasionally people who are not so nice or kind.

I wanted to write an account that captured, however imperfectly, that broader ebb and flow of my long journey, and the contemplative structure which evolved and overlaid the events which unfolded. A day by day, diary-style account seemed the best way to accomplish my aim.

There is another purpose to my writing, and that is to trigger reflection in the mind of the reader and to evoke pale shadows of the emotions of former times. If the images and thoughts I have tried to convey in the book strike a chord with the reader and bring alive again his or her own experiences, or add a new perspective to their life, it will have served its purpose.

Sigeric's Itinerary

To assist readers align my walk with Sigeric's itinerary, I have shown his stage numbers in the headings and text, for example: *Amettes to Bruay la Buissière (Sigeric stop LXXVI) (27 July)*. Bear in mind that Sigeric recorded his stages in Latin, still in common use in his day. His stage numbers start in Rome (Sigeric stop I), the reverse of my journey. Moreover, the modern Via Francigena does not pass through all of Sigeric's stops, so observant readers will notice gaps in the numbering given in my account.

Canterbury to Besançon

2012

There is an engraved concrete marker set in the lawn outside the Canterbury Cathedral which marks the official starting point of the Via Francigena. I stood there on the eve of my journey, happy that all the waiting and preparation were over. Besançon, my destination for this year, seemed an impossibly distant, almost mythical place. How would my pilgrimage unfold? Pilgrims must walk across all terrain, through all kinds of weather. Water and food might be hard to find. Sometimes we struggle and the way seems so hard, and at other times our pack seems light and we barely touch the earth. All the while, the land and the passing days write themselves into our hearts and onto our bodies.

Canterbury to Colred (July 19)

I left the Falstaff Hotel at 7 am, in cool, clear weather; with a short stop at the Cathedral to get my pilgrim passport stamped, and to wonder what lay ahead of me. Then I went into the Cathedral to chat with a few people who had gathered for prayers at that early hour. They promised to remember me at Morning Prayers, and I found it comforting to know that strangers would be thinking of me in the long days ahead.

All was quiet on the streets as I made my way through Canterbury to the open country. How exhilarating it was to leave the city behind. The sweet smell of white flowers alive with insects wafted over me. The plants bearing the white flowers on tall stalks were only weeds, but why can't weeds smell nice? The insects can't speak English, they don't know these plants are weeds; they simply love them for the food they provide. A small rabbit bounded away, it did not know I would never hurt it. Later on I saw a pile of fluffy feathers from a deadlier encounter. A cat? A fox? I heard the distant rush of motorway traffic, even deadlier.

I received a very friendly welcome from Jackie and Darryl at Colret House, Colred, at the end of my first day's walk. I sat in their tranquil garden and drank tea while writing up my notes for the day. Later, Darryl drove me to a pub at Shepherdswell for dinner among the locals. I am not sure they really believed me when I said I planned to walk across France to Switzerland. On the walk back to Colret House after my meal, I looked into a small church. It caught my attention because from a distance the flints embedded in the walls looked like oyster shells. Inside, a few people were getting ready for choir practice, or discussing church affairs, so I left quietly without disturbing them.

Colred to Calais (July 20) 2

I set out in cool, cloudy weather. Much of the route was through crops still heavy with last night's rain, dripping water onto my pants as I brushed past them on the narrow path. Part of the route was along an old Roman road. I wondered how the Romans built their roads so straight to a distant town they could not see, without compass, map or other modern surveying gear. It is easy enough to build a straight road between two inter-visible points, but what if you can't see the final destination? I did not solve the puzzle, but it was interesting to consider possible solutions that might have been available to Roman engineers.

Heavy rain descended on me as I caught my first glimpse of Dover Castle and trudged through the town to catch the Calais ferry. It was crowded with frantic, noisy activity as passengers rushed about, cramming down food and drink on the short trip to Calais. I sat in the midst of all the hubbub, with my wet rain gear dripping onto the floor.

I walked through the port at Calais and into town. I have to stay here for a second day, since accommodation at Wissant and in the surrounding area was fully booked. I would have to alter my route and walk directly to Guînes instead of following the official route. Calais was full of bustling transients, anxious to be somewhere else. The summer migration of Europeans was in full swing.

Next day I bustled about doing last-minute chores and just killing time. I was tired after a busy day and could not wait to leave Calais.

Calais to Guînes (July 22) 3

In a sense this felt like the real beginning of the Via Francigena for me. I was on the continent of Europe. I had food for lunch, a French SIM card for my phone to book accommodation, and I was ready to roll. All the complexities of planning and preparation were over. Everything had become simple and I was focussed on the journey at hand–"afoot" would be putting it better. The outside world shrank and faded away, only the journey ahead mattered.

I was disappointed to be unable to walk via Wissant, but in life we cannot always choose the path we prefer. Choices are often forced upon us and we must make the best of our lot–but never surrendering to it. Strive. Choose the difficult way. I wondered idly if it would be possible to get a boat directly from Dover to Wissant. Maybe not a commercial service, but a fishing boat or a private operator. That would more truly replicate Sigeric's journey, rather than the artificial Dover/Calais ferry and the walk along the beach to Wissant. What an exciting beginning that would be! Probably impossible with existing border controls and paranoid officials. One might be a refugee seeking to enter France illegally, like all those refugees huddling in makeshift camps at Calais trying to get to England.

Much of the walk was beside a big canal, and was very enjoyable, with cyclists and joggers out for some exercise. Men were optimistically fishing in the canal, closely watched by egrets. I heard birdsong, but not the frantic singing and activity of spring. Summer was here and efforts were now directed to getting food and raising chicks–not trying to attract a mate. Birds become boring and conservative the moment they start families. They are weighed down with responsibilities and too busy and harassed to sing anymore.

I stopped for a drink at a small café in Guînes. It was Sunday morning and the café was bustling with people and animated conversation. As new people came in they shook hands with everyone and said *"bonjour"*–even including obvious (scruffy) foreigner and outsider like me. What a lovely custom! I felt instantly at home among them–not a stranger to be mistrusted.

My stop for the day was the Auberge du Colombier. *Colombier* means "dovecote." Doves and pigeons were a survival food in the past; but squab (the same thing) is a delicacy in some countries. There were no longer any cooing pigeons in the *colombier* at my auberge, only campers packed onto the surrounding pitches as close as the pigeons once were in their little home.

Guînes to Licques (July 23)

I woke with a bad cold and felt terrible at breakfast; but it was a beautiful clear, warm day and I had to keep moving. Things did not improve during the walk. I was exceptionally tired, so I had a longer lunch stop than usual, eating my bread and cheese in a shady spot by the road. I carried an extra litre of water and even that small weight made a difference. It was uncomfortable walking over stones and piles of gravel. The piles were too wide to just step over, so it was an irritating up down, up down slog for ages.

I met another pilgrim on entering Licques, but she seemed anxious to find the parish accommodation where she planned to stay the night, so we did not chat for long.

It was quite hot when I arrived at my "chalet" at the Les Pommiers campsite, about one kilometre outside town, with an uphill climb at the end. I felt very, very tired and had to have a long afternoon nap. I was not hungry on waking, but I forced down a light dinner at the campsite café.

Today was surprisingly hard with the heat, carrying extra water and not feeling so great. I was still jet-lagged as well, after my long flight from Australia to London a few days earlier. The question was how long I would be able to keep going? I went to bed at 8 pm, so very tired, hoping to recover some strength and motivation by morning.

What's the point? Why am I so driven to do this stuff? Why not do what normal people would do and take a train to Nice and sit in cafés all day, drinking absinthe and coffee and ogling the pretty *m'selles* undulating by? Except absinthe is banned. Messes up your brain. It's messed up anyway. And absinthe makes the heart grow fonder! God–now puns! Has it come to this?

Licques to Wisques (July 24) 5

Up and at `em! Sleep is a wonderful thing. I woke motivated and ready to go again. The kind lady who ran the campsite had arranged an early breakfast for me, so I was able to start walking by 8 am. Every house and farm seemed to have frantic dogs barking at me and rushing frenziedly about their garden. The way to deal with them is to say "nice doggie" until you can find a decent rock.

I went astray on muddy, overgrown forest tracks, overgrown with nettles as well. *Don't sit among nettles to have a snack while you sort out your navigation!* I never did, of course, but others might, so it's best to sound a warning here. The problem was my GPS unit and I thought we knew better than the excellent guidebook I was carrying. GPS units can give a false sense of security in certain conditions. You still have to have situational awareness and navigate properly. It is just a tool. Like a hammer. A hammer does not build a house by itself; a carpenter has to wield it and know what he is doing.

Anyway, I blame the opinionated GPS for getting me lost; it is such a pedantic know-it-all, beeping at every turn as if I were a total idiot. "You have an OFF switch, smarty-pants GPS, so don't take that attitude with me. I can always de-Friend you!"

But it was almost worth getting lost to experience the pleasure and euphoria that I felt when I eventually got back on the right track. I might do it again. After emerging from *terra incognita*, I had lunch (baguette, cheese, dried apricots, an apple), dreaming of that wonderful cooked English breakfast at Colret House: bacon (crisp, not floppy), mushrooms, tomatoes, toast.

The path was hot and exposed after Acquin, with a couple of long, relentless climbs on bitumen roads, the heat driving up through the soles of my boots. High summer had arrived here. All the hay had been cut and rolled into big, stubby cylinders dotting the fields in regular patterns, like pieces on a gigantic chess board. Wheat was also ripening.

I arrived at my accommodation, La Sapinière, on the far side of Wisques, after a long day. I had booked it in advance, and regretted not being able to stay at the wonderful Abbey. I still felt very tired and footsore, but not as exhausted as yesterday. I drained a couple of blisters and sat in the garden, looking out over beautiful farmland and wrote my notes in the glow of late afternoon. Birds occasionally flitted from tree to tree, increasing my sense of well-being. I might make it, after all.

Wisques to Therouanne (25 July)

The Via Francigena went through open country today, mostly on roads, with a few up and downs–but nothing like the Alps that I will eventually have to cross if I am ever to reach Rome.

I had a drink and short break in a small café, everyone talking Dutch. Borders might be neat lines on a map, but cultural borders are much fuzzier–and are often defended more fiercely than physical borders.

There is a statue of St. Roch inside the church in Therouanne. He has his gourd and satchel and points to his leg, with his little dog at his side. The legend of St. Roch takes up a few paragraphs of text in Wikipedia, but its essentials are conveyed in this simple statue. Of course, you have to know the story to interpret the statue, and stories have to be written down somewhere.

Symbolism and imagery are very important. Everyone who has walked the Camino Frances and who sees a certain yellow arrow, even years later, will at once be flooded with a cascade of memories triggered by that one simple, powerful image. Like Proust and the madeleine cake in his great novel.

Even words can be powerfully symbolic. There is the literal meaning you can find in a dictionary, but there are also impressions,

15

memories and cultural images evoked by the same word that may be more compelling and evocative than the dictionary meaning. Then there is the sound and musicality of the word when it is used and spoken in different contexts. Dictionaries give you only a small part of the full meaning of a word.

I was not feeling great by the end of my walk today, so I had another early night. One does not recover from a bad cold in one day. But there is no point taking medicine to cure a cold. Remember the saying, 'If you see a doctor about a cold you can recover in seven days, otherwise it will take a week'.

Therouanne to Amettes (26 July) 7

I set out at 7 am to get my walking done in the cooler part of the day. It was very foggy all morning, with condensed mist dripping from trees and onto me. There was heavy traffic, and it was not so nice walking on busy roads with juggernauts hurtling towards me out of the mist. There was a steady, relentless climb out of Therouanne, located on the pretty River Lys. These ancient towns mean one thing: descents into valleys where the water is, followed by climbs out.

Sometimes friends ask if I ever get bored walking alone, day after day. Never! I often get lost in reflection and occasionally walk almost on autopilot. Walking provides many excellent opportunities for reflection. Apart from the joys of the natural world, one constantly sees things that are interesting. You can also ponder philosophical questions, like: what is happiness? We talk about it so frequently, and pursue it so relentlessly; but the nature of happiness is by no means a simple matter, and we often pursue empty paths towards happiness, never quite reaching it, or, if we think we have, feeling vaguely dissatisfied.

I stayed with M and Mme Gevas. They were very kind and helpful people. Mme Gevas offered to buy food for me at a supermarket when she went to do other chores. Two other walkers were also staying here, on their way to Arras, where their walk will end. We had a nice evening together until I had to toddle off to bed. Very late to bed–8:30 pm!

Amettes to Bruay la Buissière (Sigeric stop LXXVI) (27 July) 8

I said, *"Bonjour à tous"* as I walked into a busy *café-tabac* for a drink. Everyone present was intrigued that an Australian would be

16

walking across France. We had a very pleasant conversation, but when someone pressed me to have "one drink for remembrance" I knew it was time to either tear myself away, or settle in for some time. My companions were going nowhere.

The Via Francigena is not attractive here. It passes through an old mining area with a couple of huge, dark spoil heaps marking where the mine shafts were, dominating the area like small hills. An air of decline hung over everything. Someone has called these small towns "the lost villages of northern France."

My overnight stay was at "Le Cottage", some distance out of the town centre. There was no café nearby, so I shopped at the ALDI supermarket, and then went next door to buy a creamy, flaky pastry, handed to me in a beautiful little box by the *pâtissière*, as if it were a precious gift to be treasured. It was quite a challenge to prepare a meal in my small room, with no utensils. I ate straight out of the cans using the rip-off lid as a spoon; sitting on the toilet seat close to the sink in the cramped bathroom so as not to make a mess. The delicious pastry was followed by almost an entire tub of ice cream. I felt sick afterwards. What a pig!

Heavy rain and thunder burst outside as I ate, snug in my cosy room, wondering what tomorrow would bring.

Go to <u>Sigeric's Itinerary</u> for a brief explanation of Sigeric's stops shown in the headings and text.

Bruay la Buissière to Arras (Sigeric stop LXXV) (28 July)

Today was a long stage, 38 kilometres door to door according to my know-it-all GPS. Thankfully, the day was cool and the path was flat. I wanted to try a long stage as a test early in my walk, because there are more long days to come that I may not be able to avoid if accommodation is difficult to find. I was not carrying a tent, and that meant always being able to find an actual, non-fabric roof over my head each night.

The early part of the route followed the historic Chaussée Brunehaut for a short distance. It was originally a Roman road that had fallen into decay and was periodically restored in the Middle Ages. The most famous of these restorations is associated with Queen Brunhilda, which gave the road its current name. She is reputed to have been executed by dismemberment in one of the political intrigues of the period.

A cyclist on his way to Rome asked where I was going and we chatted for a bit. He insisted on posing me carefully to take my photo while I held his bike. A little too pushy, I thought. I still had a long way to go today and was anxious to push on. Quite a few pilgrims ride bikes to Rome. One certainly has more flexibility on a bike. If accommodation is hard to find, a cyclist has a bigger area in which to find alternatives.

The long day, mostly through fields of crops, seemed endless, especially the last few kilometres through the suburbs and streets of Arras.

I was very footsore and weary when I arrived at the Hostel des Trois Luppars, right on the busy main square in Arras. Another very friendly reception awaited me. "Where are the leopards?" I enquired with a smile. *"Ils sont cachée,"* was the deadpan reply. I never did find out what the deal was with the leopards.

I felt apprehensive about taking off my boots, wondering if my earlier blisters had rubbed raw. No problem, all good–just the drained blisters aching a bit. Thank god tomorrow will be a rest day for me.

My room was on the top floor, just under the sloping ceiling. I don't think I am paranoid, but I am sure my room was trying to kill me. Right next to the bed was a post that I slammed into when leaping out of bed half asleep to visit the toilet in the night. The toilet itself was tucked close under a sloping wall that I bashed my head on, in both standing and sitting positions. Staggering to the sink with multiple contusions and bending forward to wash my hands and face, my forehead slammed into another sloping wall above the sink. Best to just stay in bed and hold it in until the morning.

Arras (29 July) *10*

Arras was a very enjoyable town for a rest day, especially among the shops, cafés and the sights around the main square. Arras is very interesting historically and suffered terribly in World War One. There were several large photo albums in the Hostel des Trois Luppars, with old postcards and photos showing Arras and the main square before, during and after World War One.

Arras would make a good stop for pilgrims who have only a couple of weeks available to walk. They could walk from Calais, stay a night at the Abbey at Wisques *en route*, and then spend a week visiting some of the World War One battlefields in the region. People with family connections to explore could end their walk in an emotionally satisfying way.

Arras to Bapaume (30 July)

A cold, horrible wind sprang up in my face today and made for uncomfortable walking as it nagged me and tugged at my hat and clothing, holding me back. "Turn back," it seemed to urge me. The area is flat and open, with wind turbines on the low ridges. The Via Francigena passes between two of them. Giant scythes in the sky, reaping the wind–and sometimes mowing down passing flocks of birds. I did not see any bodies here, but apparently the toll on birdlife can be surprisingly high at some wind farms. Why can't birds avoid those huge, slow-turning blades?

I walked for a brief period in heavy rain on the very busy D7. Thankfully my poncho was a bright orange that could be seen from outer space. Quite a lot of the Via Francigena is on busy roads, and one must be very careful. I had two narrow escapes that I will describe later on.

The Via Francigena passes by a number of World War One military cemeteries on this stage; all well signposted for pilgrims who want to make a detour to visit them. The battlefields are not far distant, grim reminders of the carnage that once rolled across northern France.

I enjoyed an excellent dinner at my hotel, Le Gourmet. With a name like that, what else would one expect? This part of Bapaume is not particularly attractive.

I had recovered well on my rest day in Arras, but I was very tired again by the end of the day. The excitement of the beginning was over, the body had adjusted, minor aches and pains had settled down and my daily routine was established. I faced many more days of the same, a somewhat depressing thought. But one dare not think about the end, still so far away. I must grind out the stages, day after day, seemingly making no progress to my distant goal.

Bapaume to Peronne (31 July)

The aggravating wind was still in my face today, making the walk harder. Light rain occasionally fell from a leaden sky. I ate my lunch in the peaceful gardens of a French military cemetery near Moislans and tried to grasp what it must have been like when war raged over the land.

The soft, slanting sun in the early Flanders dawn reveals faint lines and hollows carved into the quiet fields; echoes across time of trenches, dugouts and shell holes. They grew like subterranean monsters locked in mortal struggle below a battered landscape that received the broken bodies of countless men.

The earth itself bears annual witness of the cataclysm that once wracked it, yielding up shards of men and metal from those brutal struggles. But the wounds have healed and the violent convulsions of a century ago are barely visible now in the landscape. In the sky, the larks still sing in their due season. Crops grow each year, bringing a new cycle of life into the fields of Flanders, where once was only death.

Voices of long dead men sound faintly across the vanished years, in fading photos and letters; and in the tremulous voices of those few who still remember them and mourn their passing in a distant land.

"Why stand you straight and still amid the clammy chill?"
"I stand to do you honour."
"Then remember us", the spirits whisper.
"Not as the stricken dead arrayed below,
nor as graven names upon a marble row.
But as those now living,
who surround you in the new day dawning,
far from raucous battle."
"Look into their eyes, hear their voice,
watch their bodies flow with supple grace
and you will see us live.
We lie below but still have much to give.
We are not truly dead."

A young man smiles softly at his girlfriend and hugs her briefly as she wipes her eyes, fixed on some inward, shared vision. Neither speaks as they walk among the serried graves; but in their distant gaze and youthful strength the spirits rise: shining, bright.

Peronne is an interesting town and would also make a good base for exploring World War One battlefields. There is a good museum here, as well as ample accommodation and shops.

Peaches were in full season and they were absolutely wonderful; soft and juicy, much better than the unripe peaches usually sold in big supermarkets at home. They are called stone fruit, so maybe the supermarkets think it is okay to sell them while they are still as solid as rocks.

Peronne to Trefcon (1 August) 13

It was a stiff climb out of Tertry, then open cropland swept by an unpleasant wind until I reached Trefcon, a small hamlet hidden among trees until I was almost upon it. There are no facilities in the town, apart from my accommodation at Val d'Omignon.

I knocked on the door and was welcomed by the family that owned the place. A huge dog pushed past them to greet me, very friendly once the family had approved of me. Had they not been present I might have been torn limb from limb at my first knock on the door–at least in my imagination.

Since leaving the Pas de Calais region accommodation has not been a problem, but there is a weekend coming up and a large town (St. Quentin) nearby, so maybe more problems will occur as the locals pour into the country for a break.

Trefcon to Seraucourt le Grand (Sigeric stop LXXIII) (2 August) 14

It was too far to walk from Trefcon to Tergnier in one day, so I stopped roughly halfway at Seraucourt le Grand, at Camping du Vivier aux Carpes. Trees and water surrounded the busy campsite. The facilities were excellent and the owners very efficient and helpful. They tried to find me accommodation for later in my walk.

I had a cosy little caravan by the water to relax in and make my temporary home. I made tea and sat in a chair under the awning and watched the comings and goings of other holiday makers.

I chatted with another new arrival who had driven more than 400 kilometres that day and would drive to Calais tomorrow. That is quite normal when driving in a car on autoroutes, but I was astonished nevertheless. After many days of walking stages of about 25 kilometres per day, my horizons had shrunk and it seemed remarkable to me that this person would cover effortlessly and comfortably in a few hours, a journey that had taken me many arduous days. Tomorrow, when I arrived at Tergnier, he would probably be relaxing at home in England. He seemed quite unimpressed with my walk from Calais. Drivers don't have the perspective of walkers. On an autoroute a driver will cover 25 kilometres in 12 minutes, a mere blink of an eye, and in the utmost comfort; with music, air conditioning, food and drink to hand, chatting to companions lolling at their ease.

Seraucourt le Grand to Laon (Sigeric stop LXXII) (3 August)

15

Today (Friday) my luck ran out for accommodation and I had to take the train from Tergnier to Laon because it was too far to continue walking that day. The 36-kilometre Tergnier to Laon stage was a problem, with very limited half-way accommodation other than at Cessières. But Cessières was all booked, and nothing else was available near the Via Francigena route.

Weekends near big towns like Laon, St. Quentin, Reims are problematical in the summer holiday season because local people also walk and want to get out into the country. Fortunately, there are convenient train stations along the Via Francigena, giving pilgrims more options if accommodation is difficult to find.

It was so disappointing to have to take a train and miss stages when I had set my heart on walking the entire Via Francigena. Another option would have been to take a taxi to stay somewhere for the night, and return by taxi to the same spot to continue walking next day.

Laon to Reims (Sigeric stop LXX) (4 August)

16

More accommodation problems occurred ahead of me, so spent the morning looking around Laon and took the train to Reims.

Reims Cathedral is a major tourist attraction, and is important in the history of France. The kings of France were crowned there. It was built on the site of Roman baths. Many early Christian churches were built over Roman and other pagan sites.

I listened to beautiful, soft singing by an impromptu choir in the crowded nave of the Cathedral; the voices harmonising wonderfully with the resonances of the large space. As soon as the singing ceased, the group dispersed among the crowd and were quickly swallowed up. Only the memory of their music remained. After a few moments of quiet reflection, the listeners also dispersed and the buzz of conversation once more filled the Cathedral.

I will stay another day in Reims to see as much as I can. The Via Francigena takes its toll on body and mind and the downtime will help me to regain strength after my cold. I need the company of other people for a while and it will be pleasant just hanging out here and chatting to people.

Reims to Trepail (6 August)

The television at breakfast announced that Curiosity, the Mars Science Laboratory launched by NASA, has landed on the Red Planet! What an inspiring achievement. Who has not looked up with wonder at stars splashed across the sky, yearning to know what is out there. We gaze at a star and wonder, does it have planets? Is there some being out there who is also looking into the firmament with equal wonder? If only we could meet! Or at least know that we both exist.

It was a lovely walk along a big canal for a kilometre or so out of Reims. I saw a familiar scallop shell sign where the St. Jacque de Compostelle route to Santiago shares the Via Francigena for a little distance, until the Via Francigena turned away from the canal into open country; final destination Rome.

The country changed completely after Les Puits. Suddenly I was among rolling fields covered with vines in serried ranks all the way to the horizon. Champagne to go with my lobster for my *al fresco* (and imaginary) lunch! Even the small villages tucked in the hollows seemed to be different to the earlier lost villages of northern France. The French accent was also changing. It was exciting to be entering new lands. Curiosity! It's one reason we go on pilgrimages.

Mme Jacqueminet ran the gîte where I stayed at Trepail. She was very helpful and made accommodation bookings for me for the next couple of nights. She has the key to the church next door and showed me around. I glanced inside the Confessional booth and was surprised to see that it was being used as a storage closet for brooms and other cleaning materials. Presumably the local population were not in need of Confession.

Trepail to Châlons en Champagne (Sigeric stop LXIX) (7 August)

The route out of Trepail descended all the way to Ambonnay and suddenly there were no more vines, only crops, fields of hay and a few sunflowers. Presumably the soils and climate of the higher ground are better for grapes.

There was another nice walk along a canal for quite a few kilometres into Châlons en Champagne. Boats plied the canal, returning my greetings. Hopeful fishermen lined the banks. Canals are wonderful for walkers. The path is naturally flat and there is usually good shade.

My pack was lighter, with only one kilogram of water to carry, and walking felt really easy today. On days like this I floated over the earth; but on other days I plodded along with the pack a lead weight dragging me down. So far the weather has been good; warm but not hot. But at some point the dreaded *vague de chaleur* was poised to strike France.

Châlons en Champagne has all facilities a weary walker requires and plenty of interesting things to see. I learned that Attila the Hun's ruthless advance into Europe was halted at the Battle of Châlons in 451. Help for pilgrims is available at Saint Etienne's Cathedral, the UNESCO-listed Church of Notre Dame en Vaux, and the Tourist Office.

I often visited the *Offices du Tourisme* in France and was always impressed by the services they provided. On one occasion I emailed for an accommodation list and received a comprehensive reply setting out what was available in the area. Even in economically difficult times the French seem willing to continue with services that would have been ruthlessly cut back, or privatised, in other countries.

Châlons en Champagne to Coole (8 August) 3

Most of the route is on the Voie Romaine, cutting through rolling farmland, as straight as a ruler. The Voie Romaine is extremely exposed today and uncomfortably stony underfoot. It would be very unpleasant to walk along it in cold, wet weather.

Western Europe was once covered with forests, unlike the open farmland modern pilgrims encounter. During Roman times, clearings were cut in the forests to grow crops and raise livestock. In the Middle Ages more forests were cut for fuel, agriculture and building. During the Age of Exploration that followed, more forests were cut to build expanding cities and the ships that sailed to all parts of the world. In fact, the first energy crisis occurred when wood for fuel became scarce, spurring the rise of coal.

The Via Francigena still passes through occasional forested areas. Most are relatively young, but there are a few remnants of old forest left. It's worth paying attention to them to get an idea of the lands Sigeric would have travelled through: heavily wooded in many places and sparsely populated. The climate was also different at that time.

At Fontaine sur Coole (Sigeric stop LXVIII), the route descended into a small forested valley, wonderfully sheltered and cool after walking through open farmland. As soon as I arrived at any of

Sigeric's stops it became obvious why villages grew up in those places: good water supplies and shelter from harsh weather. One sometimes finds a *rue du Moulin* in small river-side towns, even though the water mill has long since disappeared.

I received a wonderful welcome from Jean-Pierre and Monique into their family at Coole. They run a working farm and Monique also works in a local *Mairie*, so there was no one home when I arrived. I relaxed in the garden and did a few chores until Jean-Pierre arrived home. I had dinner with them and some of their relatives who they had invited over to dinner. We enjoyed a very nice evening *en famille*.

Coole to le Meix-Tiercelin (9 August)   4

All of today's short stage was on the exposed and hot Voie Romaine. Shortly after leaving Coole, I met a farm worker walking to his fields. He was surprised to see me and was very interested in my long walk. Jean-Paul also came by in his tractor and stopped for a chat. I was so pleased to see him again. He offered me a ride into the next town, but I had to refuse. I must be strong and never accept lifts.

Le Meix-Tiercelin was a small village and Mme Collombar's gîte was the only place to stay. She prepared an excellent dinner, including soup! I still had no accommodation for tomorrow night (Friday), so I expected I would have a long walk to look forward to. The *meteo* says tomorrow will be hot, and that means carrying extra water again.

le Meix-Tiercelin to Brienne le Château (10 August)   5

I had no luck finding accommodation, so I walked 34 kilometres to Brienne today. I passed sunflowers, but facing away from the sun–why? Then a field of lavender appeared, like bright paint splashed across the land and giving off a wonderful aroma in the warm air.

The last six kilometres into Brienne le Château were horrible. The road was being resurfaced with gravel and bitumen, making for unpleasant walking: noisy, hot and dusty; with flying gravel thrown up by traffic passing on the new surface. The whole process of trucks arriving and waiting their turn to spread gravel, the spreading of the gravel and then spraying on the bitumen was remarkably coordinated and efficient. I was surprised by how fast the job advanced: at a good walking pace, so I was only slowly able to outpace the juggernaut. It would have been a breeze for soldiers of the Roman Empire. Roman marching speeds were remarkable: 30 kilometres in five hours, or, when forced-marching, almost 40 kilometres in the same time. And that was carrying a heavy load.

I wonder how long the Romans took to build their fantastic roads? Because they followed the most efficient routes, Roman roads are often the basis of many modern roads. If a walker encounters a long stretch of perfectly straight road, it is a good bet that it was once a Roman road.

Brienne le Château to Bar sur Aube (Sigeric stop LXV) (11 August) *6*

I woke tired and not motivated after yesterday's long, hot walk. I just wanted to sleep in and take the day off, but I had to trudge 29 kilometres today.

A *boulanger's* van was driving around one of the small villages I passed through (it was Saturday morning), blowing its horn from time to time. The locals came out in slippers and even dressing gowns to buy fresh bread and to briefly gossip. Country *boulangers* are disappearing, forcing people in small villages to go further afield for their bread. This trend was spoken of with regret. Something important is lost when age-old customs die out.

The process of change is one of the things I noticed on the Via Francigena. Churches and wayside crosses were often almost derelict because they are no longer valued in a secular society with dwindling church attendance, so there is no money for restoration. Many small villages are also succumbing to social and economic change. I often walked through hamlets without seeing a single human being. A sense of encroaching abandonment was often pervasive. Later on during my walk, I came upon a small hamlet that actually had been abandoned, the stone houses tumbling into ruins. But in was not all depressing. In other small villages, new houses were being built and an air of renewal existed. The contrast was inexplicable to a pilgrim passing through.

The great forces of change are rarely apparent within a single lifetime. We think the future will be an extension of the present. The Romans who travelled the Voie Romaine no doubt thought their world would endure far into the future. Sigeric's world probably seemed unchanging to him, yet it was vastly different to the Roman world of centuries earlier and would, in its turn, pass away; swallowed up by the implacable future.

One thing that never changes is the fundamental nature of human beings: the search for meaning in our lives, the desire to be loved, and to know that our labours are valued. Giving and belonging. Courage to face the trials we all must endure, but which have the power to ennoble even the most humble of us.

Much of the walk was along the River Aube, with holiday-makers enjoying themselves on the bank and swimming in the river, thankfully oblivious to the forces of history closing in on them.

Bar sur Aube to Clairvaux sur Aube (12 August) ⊐

It was a beautiful walk out of Bar sur Aube, followed by a very stiff climb on roads and tracks among vines, and finally through a large forest to Clairvaux. The Hôtel l'Abbaye at Clairvaux has a restaurant, a *café-tabac* and a shady garden to relax in. It was said to be often busy with people visiting relatives or friends in the abbey prison.

The abbey has been a prison since the days of Napoleon. It was founded in 1115 AD by Saint Bernard as a Cistercian monastery. Despite being a prison, it was listed in 1926 as an historical monument. Today, very restricted access is allowed for guided tours. Prison rules require visitors to hand in their passports before going on a tour of the 'open' part of the complex.

The site and the buildings have huge potential as a major attraction like, for example, Tintern Abbey in the UK—if only the prison authorities would loosen their grip. Some restoration was in progress when I was there, but it was very limited. Much of the interior decoration had become very dilapidated. It is a pity that such an important site in the monastic history of Western Europe has been so neglected.

There were problems with accommodation at Châteauvillain and Mormant, my next two stops, so I had to take a rest day at Clairvaux to work out what to do. Mormant was the main problem and the alternatives seemed to be either Leffonds or Villers sur Suize; both involving detours away from the Via Francigena. The lady at the Abbey visitor's centre was very helpful researching accommodation options and gave me a sheaf of computer printouts to pore over.

Clairvaux sur Aube to Châteauvillain (14 August) 8

It was a very pleasant, easy walk to Châteauvillain. There were big trucks with huge loads of hay on the roads; but they were slow and presented no danger. It was high summer now, very different to when I started in rainy England several weeks ago.

The early harvests were being brought in and farmers were already preparing for winter, as they have done for millennia. We take our food supply for granted today. The supermarkets are always full of everything we need. Famine was a constant fear in Europe up until the early 19th century. But the last great famines of the world were in India, China and the Ukraine in the 20th century, when many millions died.

At the time of Sigeric, villagers and farmers lived in almost constant fear of famine. If the rain did not come at the right time, crops would fail. Disease might destroy them. Even when crops had ripened and were ready for harvest, a sudden storm or pestilence might destroy them in a moment. One understands why farmers and villagers celebrated with harvest festivals and church blessings when the harvested crops were safe in their granaries and store houses. It meant survival over winter was assured.

I stayed in the refuge for pilgrims. It was only a short walk from the *Mairie*, where I collected the keys. The refuge was small, but quite comfortable. It even provided coffee and basic breakfast foodstuffs. There was no shower only a sink with cold water. There was a microwave to heat food and water. I found a mini-mart close to the refuge where I bought food and drink for dinner. There was a big heater in the room for cold days. There was no shower, but I suppose if you arrived at the *Mairie* dripping and bedraggled, looking woebegone, someone might take pity on you and find a shower somewhere else.

The church at Châteauvillain was badly decaying inside, but I could still see that the stained glass windows and remnants of a ceiling fresco must have been quite impressive at one time. There were lots of amusing street signs in the town, apparently put up with the approval of the town officials. The *Bureau de Vote* (the office where citizens voted in elections) had a sign on the door showing a flock of sheep. I wonder who was responsible for such officially-sanctioned levity.

I was alone in the refuge and whiled away the time after dinner by reading the visitor's book. A previous pilgrim had written that he was feeling lonely. It is true that the Via Francigena does not attract the large numbers of pilgrims who walk the Camino de Santiago de Compostela. So far I had met only one walking pilgrim, although quite a few cyclists passed me.

Personally, I did not mind the solitude. It allowed me to reflect and to attune myself to the natural beauty of the land I was walking through. There were always wonders to see that might easily be missed if chatting with a companion. Small flowers and intricate plants often grew along the verges of the path. Tiny creatures rustled among them. They could all be easily missed if I was not attuned to the landscape.

Châteauvillain to Villers sur Suize (15 August) 9

Today I had to detour away from the Via Francigena to find accommodation at Villers sur Suize. The Gîte de Groupe directly on the main route at Mormant was full, so I could not stay there.

Much of today's stage was through the large Forêt de Châteauvillain. I emerged into open country with that annoying headwind back to harass me.

Mormant was nothing special to look at so far as the abbey ruins were concerned. Having seen it, I would not choose to stay there, except out of necessity. Leffonds, a five kilometre walk from Mormant, had more facilities and turned out to be more interesting. Even better for a weary walker, the final approach was down a steep valley, quite pretty.

I continued on to the Auberge de la Fontaine at Villers sur Suize, where I stayed for the night. The staff were very busy serving lunch to holiday makers and day trippers when I arrived. I sat at a table among them to have a snack and write my notes until my room was ready. It was such a pleasant spot that I arranged to have an early pilgrim dinner there that evening.

The room was very comfortable, with a good bed that didn't bend me like a banana, or tilt alarmingly to one side as I slept, or poke sharp springs into my flesh. I could write a lengthy book on "How I Survived the Beds of the Via Francigena".

So my detour off the Via Francigena proved to be a pleasant diversion. How often it is the case that unplanned events which seem irksome at the time turn out to be very welcome experiences. It brought home to me once again that the unknown and its imagined difficulties are not always to be feared. Positive outcomes often occur if we are brave enough to take the difficult way.

Villers sur Suize to Langres (16 August) 10

There was also a shop in the Auberge selling food and fresh bread that opened at 6:30 am–very convenient for early starters like me. Much of today's walk was through beautiful, rolling countryside, especially in the morning. The recommended Via Francigena route from Beauchemin to Langres was on the very busy D3. I took an alternative route on small, quiet roads via St. Martin lès Langres. It had only one steep descent into a river valley with an old water mill still preserved, followed by the inevitable steep ascent out of the valley.

My first view of Langres was a little daunting. It sits on a hilltop (like Laon) with a long, relentless climb to reach the town.

I stayed at the Hôtel l'Europe in Langres and enjoyed very good meals, with fast service for my early pilgrim dinner. I preferred to go to bed early each night so I could arise early and complete my day's walking in the cooler part of the day.

There was a sense now that my journey to Besançon was coming to an end, with only six more walking days—if all goes well.

Every ending contains both joy and sadness; joy at having endured the inevitable hardships of a long walk and at having met with kindness on the way; but sadness at having reached an end and realising it is not enough, and never will be enough, while there is life and strength to seek what lies beyond the next hill. In some sense many of us are only truly alive when we embark with hope upon a difficult undertaking with an uncertain outcome. It's one reason long pilgrimages are so addictive.

The next stage to Champlitte is more than 39 kilometres, so I want to break it at Les Archots, where there is only one gîte. The location and owner (Serge Francois) were reported to be very pilgrim-friendly, so I particularly want to stay there. But to get a booking I had to spend another day at Langres.

Langres to les Archots (18 August)

Hot days lie ahead as the threatened heat wave is about to strike France. Today's forecast was for 34 degrees Celsius, but it will be hotter walking on the road. It was already very warm when I set out at 7 am.

The Gîte les Archots is close to the small Pont des Archots, off the road and among trees. There is no hamlet here, just the gîte and a few other buildings. All rooms were full (it was Saturday) and nine of us sat down to dinner. And what a wonderful dinner! Many courses and excellent presentation. Good company. Wine. Excellent hospitality from the Francois family. None of the other guests were walking the Via Francigena, they were just out in the country for the weekend.

Tomorrow was expected be very hot as the heat wave grips France, especially in the south, but not even the north of the country will escape. There was heavy coverage of the *vague de chaleur* on TV. Everyone was urged to avoid strenuous exercise, to stay indoors in a cool place and to drink plenty of water. The concern was understandable. There were over 14,000 heat-related deaths in a catastrophic heat wave in the summer of 2003. Another heat wave in 2006 destroyed many crops on the eve of harvesting. Thankfully much of the route to Champlitte is through forest, which should give some shade.

Les Archots to Champlitte (19 August) 12

I left early so as to arrive in Champlitte before the worst heat of the afternoon. Serge pressed fruit and drinks on me as I said goodbye.

There is a church and cemetery at Grenant (Sigeric stop LXII) where potable water is available. Churches with cemeteries will always have a water supply. I refreshed myself under the water before setting out on the stiff 45-minute climb out of the valley. The path then passes through open farmland to Champlitte.

By noon a hot wind was blowing and it was very unpleasant walking on the exposed road, with waves of heat buffeting me. The last 90 minutes into Champlitte were pretty horrible, but fortunately it was mostly downhill. The receptionist in my hotel at Champlitte said it was 38 degrees Celsius outside. I lay on the bed under a wet towel to cool down and drank copious amounts of water. My room was directly under the roof and it remained hot all night.

Heat exhaustion is a possibility when walking with a load in very hot conditions. I wore a broad-brimmed hat, long, loose-fitting pants and a loose, long-sleeved shirt. The idea is to minimise direct contact of the sun on bare skin, while allowing air to circulate near the body. Dress like a Tuareg! Desert dwellers have worked out how to survive in such a harsh environment, and are always swathed in cloth. Don't hurry! That will simply make you sweat more and become exhausted.

As for water, I found that my own experience was probably a better guide than generic rules about how much to drink. Two litres from my pack and 750ml at the Grenant cemetery were fine for me today, and I probably drank another 750ml in the hour after arriving at the hotel and more at dinner.

Two pilgrims *en route* to Rome arrived at 5:30 pm after having walked 39 kilometres from Langres. They were experienced walkers who said they normally walked thirty or more kilometres per day; but even so, I thought it was unwise on such a hot day. Both were noticeably underweight, the woman almost cadaverous. At least there were two of them to support each other.

13

Champlitte to Dampierre sur Salon (20 August)

It was exceptionally hot and humid today and I was soaked with sweat by mid-morning. My water intake rose quickly in such conditions. I stopped in the cool shade of the church at Delain to replenish my water and have a snack.

Summer was well advanced here, and the heat wave was rapidly drying moisture from the crops. All the hay had been cut and the bare fields were already sprouting new growth. Corn was fully grown, but the cobs had not matured yet. Grape picking should start in a few weeks.

Soon autumn and winter will come and the land will sleep, husbanding its dormant strength until the next spring awakening. Pilgrims too will have found their own rest over winter, awaiting the new year to set forth once more on a quest that has no ending, only a new beginning.

My Hôtel de la Tour in Dampierre was on the 7th floor of a boxy, modern glass-clad building, completely different to any other place I had stayed at on the Via Francigena. The rooms had balconies where one could survey the town. There was a *boulanger* on the ground floor, and a big supermarket across the road, so supplies for next day were close to hand.

It rained in the late afternoon, with occasional thunder grumbling in the distance. The weather seemed to be changing, so hopefully the heat wave will soon be over.

I was self-conscious about wearing flip-flops to dinner, although I was the only one present, and took care to hide my feet under the table, out of the gaze of the immaculate waiter.

A noisy tour group arrived late, as I was going to bed, calling to each other as they searched for their rooms, slamming doors, dragging bulging suitcases, flushing toilets. Tour groups inhabit (infest?) a parallel universe, but unfortunately their universe is not sound-proofed. I must have looked alarming to them as I suddenly appeared in the doorway semi-naked and asked if they could be a little quieter, because I needed to sleep. Unfortunately, we did not seem to share a common language, so I fled back into my room.

Dampierre sur Salon to Gy (21 August)

There was a long climb out of Dampierre, the first of several long uphill slogs during the day. None of them were steep, just relentless.

I was almost struck by an overtaking truck that passed within a metre of me early in the morning. The driver was probably so intent on overtaking the line of traffic safely, and watching for oncoming traffic, that he may not have even seen me. Maybe the low morning sun was in his eyes as well. I had to stop for a few moments to compose myself. I always walked facing oncoming traffic, but that does not protect one from overtaking vehicles approaching from behind. Shortly afterwards I came across two roadside shrines to the victims of traffic accidents on this section of the D5. Why was it so dangerous here? It was not obvious to a stranger like me passing through, but it must be to the locals.

Seveux (Sigeric stop LXI) is an interesting village, close to the broad River Saône. The official Via Francigena route tries to include most, if not all, of Sigeric's stops. Occasionally pilgrims have to make a short detour to pass through a particular Sigeric stop. I was always interested to see them where convenient and to muse over what those villages would have been like in the 10th century.

Later I came to a small village called Madelaine, and recalled Proust's great novel *"A la Recherche du Temps Perdu."* It begins with the smell of a madelaine cake, which triggers a cascade of memories for Proust.

I had a lunch stop at La Chapelle St. Quillain. There were picnic tables with seats in a small shady park, with rubbish bins for the remains of my lobster and empty champagne bottles. Unfortunately, the lobster tasted like bread and cheese, and the champagne like water! But I could imagine what such a feast would have tasted like. There was a restored *lavoir* here, but the water point was signed "not potable." *Lavoirs* were communal washing places that were once common in France. They were sited on rivers or over a spring and were often roofed to provide shelter for the washerwomen. Some *lavoirs* were quite elaborate and many are being restored. A few date from the 10th century.

The last eight kilometres into Gy were hot and horrible, on a long straight road. Straight, flat roads are the worst for walking, because one looks ahead and the way seems endlessly long and boring. Whereas on bendy roads there is always some anticipatory interest in seeing what lies beyond the next curve.

The Hôtel Pinocchio at Gy was close to the Via Francigena route and very comfortable, with a rejuvenating swimming pool. There was no restaurant for dinner, but there was one next door which served fast, friendly meals and excellent pizza.

There was a storm late in the afternoon, with light rain and thunder. Then a cool breeze sprang up, hopefully marking the end of the heat wave for this year.

Gy to Geneuille (22 August)   15

I had a long, relentless climb out of Gy, but there were picnic tables and seats at the top for a break. The route along the D66, through the beautiful Bois de Gy, made a very enjoyable walk. The countryside was getting much hillier now, which made for very pretty vistas.

Trees were being felled in the forest and huge stacks of logs lay along the route, ready for collection. It seemed to be well managed by selective felling, so the forest still looked quite intact, not like the brutalised landscapes that one sees in so many other parts of the world. Thankfully, logging practices in Europe seem to be more sympathetic to the environment and more sustainable.

The heat wave was over, but it was still very hot in the afternoon. The last few very hot days were quite draining, but the stages have been mercifully short.

I stopped at Geneuille for the night so as to have only a short, pleasurable walk–a sort of triumphal progress—into Besançon tomorrow. I stayed at the beautiful Château de la Dame Blanche, set among trees and gardens. The reception staff seemed a little put off by my rather dishevelled appearance and I felt a bit uncomfortable. I had a very good room (with air conditioning!), set and park-like surroundings, but too far out of the actual village for shopping.

Then I set about emptying every superfluous item from my pack. All the extra food was eaten. I threw away one of my empty plastic bottles of water. Out went scraps of paper and assorted bits of useful rubbish. I wanted to float over the ground tomorrow with the lightest load possible.

I ate in the hotel that evening, but the waiter apparently thought I was a bit too scruffy for their excellent restaurant and might be embarrassed. He placed me as unobtrusively as possible in the full room. That was a kind gesture.   16

Geneuille to Besançon (Sigeric stop LIX) (23 August)

After an excellent breakfast at the Château, I hit the road at 7:30 am in cool conditions. There was a stiff climb soon after leaving

Geneuille, but after that it was a very enjoyable walk to Besançon. My route through Besançon wound through endless suburbs, back streets and major road works to the Hôtel Florel, next to the train station. I simply followed the beeps of my GPS unit, with hardly any idea of where I actually was at any moment.

Journey's end for 2012.

It seemed so far in the past, in an almost mythical age, that I had set out alone from Canterbury on an uncertain journey. The Via Francigena can be intimidating for a solo pilgrim, and I was assailed by fears throughout my journey.

But I need not have worried. There were so many kind people along the way. I experienced quiet, matter-of-fact kindness that sought no reward and was just the decency of ordinary people towards a tired, transient stranger from another country, far from home. A restless seeker who must have puzzled them sometimes, whose eyes seemed forever fixed on a distant horizon.

My thoughts went back to those kind people who said a prayer for me in the great Cathedral at Canterbury all those weeks ago.

I took the TGV back to Paris, and the Eurostar to London. I sat transfixed at the window, desperately trying to catch a glimpse of the places where I had walked. On the unfolding map in my mind I inched across Europe as slowly as a caterpillar inches along a twig. But the unstoppable train hurtled through the countryside, leaving me with only a jumbled kaleidoscope of memories and images of the land; and satisfaction tinged with regret and even sadness. The past can never be recovered, no matter how much we yearn to relive the loves and pleasures of former days. Perhaps we should not even try; looking instead to the future and the prospect of joys still to come.

o o o

Photographs

Photo 1: A British War Cemetery on the Via Francigena after leaving Arras.

Photo 2: The Via Francigena after leaving Licques.

Photo 3: One of the numerous crosses that pilgrims encounter on the Via Francigena. This one seems to have been well cared for, with flower pots and perhaps even a fresh coat of paint. Sadly, others have fallen into disrepair.

Besançon to Vercelli

2013

My thoughts were never far from the Via Francigena as I waited at home and planned for my return to Besançon in the summer of 2013. It was some reassurance having completed a large part of the journey, but no long walk can be taken for granted. This year I would face new challenges, including crossing the Swiss Alps.

Besançon (June 17)

On my return to Besançon I found the city to be still a work in progress. The streets were still in a chaos of construction as the new tram line was being installed. Residents complained in the local paper about noise and disruption.

The kebab café near the train station where I ate and chatted with the owner last year, a respectable Turkish man, had now closed down with no trace whatever left of its former life; only cold, anonymous metal shutters faced the street. What had become of him? Why did his life change so that he left his shop? Did better opportunities arise for him elsewhere, or did the relentless force of economic pressure drive him out of business? People always have to eat, especially all those ravenous young backpackers pouring through the busy train station; and kebabs are quick and cheap. Business should have been good. All things change, and we have to accept it; but changes that upend the lives of ordinary people make me feel sad and powerless.

Tomorrow I will start on the journey to Vercelli, the next section of my Via Francigena. Another leap into the unknown, the looming Pass at the Col Grand St. Bernard through snaggle-tooth mountains always in the back of my mind. The Pass was also a big psychological divide. Once over it, the way would be downhill, the challenge of the mountains met. All would be easy after the Pass!

How often do we say to ourselves, I will be happy if I win the lottery or if some other dream comes true? But success always seems to sow the seeds of a vague discontent, a yearning for something more that can't quite be grasped. Perhaps that is the eternal lot of mankind, the force that drove our early ancestors out of Africa to occupy every corner of the Earth, to go to the Moon, and to unravel some of the deepest secrets of nature.

Besançon to Trépot (June 18)

Today was Deborah's day. After taking a picture on the outskirts of Besançon I turned around to walk on, and there she was, smiling, with her heavy pack—"I can get more in my new one," she told me later. It was Day One for me this year, but Day "Many" for Deborah, who had started in Canterbury weeks ago.

We walked together and chatted, I gradually learned how remarkable she was. Deborah was on a mission, totally committed to her amazing dream. She was walking the world to spread a message of love. Not in a hippie sense, but in a practical way, by encouraging people she met to perform simple acts of love in their daily lives by writing a small promise in her notebook. None of us alone can change the world, but the simple actions of many people can make a difference.

Deborah had left her home and burnt her bridges; such was her faith in her mission. Bridges burnt so that stronger ones could be built to a better world. The big thing is to try, to have faith; to hope that even one of us can make an impact, however small. She had completed many of the famous long distance walks, including the Israel National Trail from south to north—much of it through desert. "I carried 6 litres of water sometimes," she mentioned in passing.

Eventually our paths diverged; we hugged and wished each other well. I shed a few tears afterwards, and loneliness gripped me in its familiar dark embrace. People slip through our hands who should have been cherished better. Far too often in our lives we take our families and friends for granted, and when it comes to say our final goodbyes we have no time left to make up for the omissions of the past.

Trépot to Aubonne (June 19)

Today was a hot day, but the heat had not yet burnt away the lush growth of late spring. Hay had been cut and dotted the fields in the same giant rolls I had seen last year. But where were the birds? The countryside seemed so quiet, without the frantic birdsong of spring.

Pushing through a field of tall grass sent pollen flying in clouds of wispy smoke, covering everything. My water bottles looked as if they had been dusted with talcum powder. Enough pollen coated my clothes and pack to ensure days of red-eyed sneezing to come.

Farm dogs of indeterminate savagery ran barking at me, and I was bereft of even a walking pole for defence, until an old lady called them off–then offered me fresh water, hurrying indoors to fetch it.

Aubonne to Pontarlier (Sigeric stop LVII) (20 June)

Today began with ominous dark clouds and rumbles of thunder, and not long after I started walking the skies opened with snapping cracks of thunder and deluging rain. Fortunately I was passing through a small village that gave me some shelter from the torrent. The storm passed quickly and in an hour I was walking through country that was quite dry.

Later I came to confusing forest paths caused by fresh logging and machinery. In Sigeric's day travellers had other fears in the dark primeval forests of Europe: there might be robbers, and perhaps they also feared malign pre-Christian spirits. A holy man like Sigeric would have had no truck with malign spirits, although the early Church certainly integrated good pagan places and beliefs into their faith where expedient. It was a case of "if you can't beat them, join them," at least to a certain extent.

I decided to follow the larger and older track, even though my GPS unit showed it was taking me steadily away from the next waypoint. I pressed on, hoping that the path would eventually loop back towards the waypoint, which it did. GPS units are a great aid to peace of mind when navigating, but what they tell you requires interpretation. A GPS compass shows the direction to the next waypoint in a straight line, regardless of how the path might twist and turn as you walk to that waypoint. On a very loopy path the compass might sometimes show you to be walking directly away from the waypoint. Very disconcerting until you realise what is happening! With an accurate map, on the other hand, you can see the big picture and all is obvious. A GPS unit can also lead to unwise over-confidence, but that is a salutary story for later in my pilgrimage.

Pontarlier to Jougne (21 June)

The mountains were getting closer. I will be in Switzerland tomorrow! I sat on a wayside seat perfectly placed to capture wonderful views in the morning light. Jagged hills rose before me with golden sunlight painting the tips of rocky ridges. Behind me was the rounded valley I had already walked through that morning. The sun had not yet penetrated into every corner and the valley was still swathed in dim, misty light. Later on I walked softly on dappled forest paths beside a rushing stream of clear, cold water. The little stream would soon join other streams, and finally enter the mighty

Rhône River; which would empty into the distant Mediterranean Sea.

How different it was from the flat lands far to the west which I had crossed last year. Thinking back, those days and places were a jumble of impressions. Only the people I met and who took me in for the night and gave me a meal stood out, like havens in a storm-wracked sea. Memories overlap over time, some becoming stronger, others fading; but all of them changing. Each recalled memory is a subjective reconstruction of an imagined past, coloured by all the emotions of that time, as well as the emotions of later times.

"Yesterday is but a dream and tomorrow is only a vision, but today well-lived makes every yesterday a dream of happiness and every tomorrow a vision of hope." (Sanskrit verse).

Jougne to Orbe (22 June)

I crossed into Switzerland via a small country track with only a few cows and their tinkling bells to check my passport and to welcome me into a new country. I had imagined I would pass through a normal customs and immigration control point with bored officials staring at me, not farmyard animals. This is the new Europe. I like it.

Today was a very pleasant walk, with lots of country paths; forests to get lost in, with a tangle of route signs at one ambiguous fork; an autoroute arcing across a valley; the remains of a Roman road. There was even a very good model of a Spanish galleon in a small public plot of garden by the roadside. So often on the Via Francigena I came across incongruous things like that, which seemed so out of place that I yearned to know their stories.

Orbe to Echallens (23 June)

I had to detour to Echallens, away from the official Via Francigena route, to get accommodation and to optimise subsequent stage distances. The receptionist and a patron at my hotel yesterday were very helpful in finding me a motel at Echallens, on the main road out of Echallens to Yverdon (Sigeric stop LVI)).

There was a cold wind at times today. Weekend cyclists and runners were out and about. I passed a busy golf course. Strawberry pickers were filling their little buckets among the strawberry plants, with children calling excitedly to one another as they searched for the luscious fruit among the foliage. Ripening fields of grain spread across the land.

Echallens to Cully (24 June)

There are two obvious routes from Echallens back to the Via
Francigena; a direct route along the main road, and a longer one on
smaller country roads. I chose the shorter main road despite its
heavy traffic, because I wanted to reach Cully today and make up
time lost on earlier stages. Large tractor-driven mowers were cutting
grass on both sides of the road, causing traffic to back up in both
directions, with frequent impatient overtaking. I had to be aware
constantly of dangers from behind. Steady rain was falling and
visibility was not good. It was a very unpleasant experience having
impatient drivers pressing close upon me. I had one close shave
until I got back to the Via Francigena and onto quiet roads and
paths.

I reached Lausanne (Sigeric stop LIV) as the rain stopped and the
sky cleared. Lausanne would be a wonderful place to explore, but I
had no interest in visiting the sights. But I was certainly interested
in having a large bowl of spaghetti, with salad and endless amounts
of bread at a café near the cathedral. The girls who served me made
sure I was well fed, glancing curiously at me when I called for more
and more bread.

The remainder of the walk through endless boring suburbia was
horrible until a brief (steep!) excursion up into the vineyards just
before Cully; with wonderful views down to the lake and across to
the mountains. More vineyards awaited me next day.

Lausanne is a popular starting point for those who want to walk
part of the Via Francigena but have limited time. The first two days
along the lake are quite flat and allow the body to adjust easily to
walking long distances. There are wonderful lake and mountain
views. Ample facilities exist for eating, accommodation and
shopping. You could even add variety and interest by taking one of
the frequent ferries that connect towns on the lake.

Cully to Villeneuve (25 June)

Neat vineyards swept down to the lake, carrying the eye across
rippling water to snowy mountain tops. The grapes were just out of
flower; with tiny bunches of pinhead-sized fruit dotting the vines.
Workers were busy pruning back vigorous foliage to expose the
grapes to life-giving sunlight. It was an incredibly lovely, timeless
scene; well worth the climb from the lakeside road.

Today was probably the loveliest walk I have done so far on the
Via Francigena; with lake views, shady paths and glimpses across

the lake to mountains at every step. There are many seats if you want to relax for a moment and savour everything–and perhaps to recall other lakes and other peaceful moments.

Villeneuve to St. Maurice (Sigeric stop LI) (26 June)

The Via Francigena finally left the Lake at Villeneuve and headed up the Rhône valley into mountains that loomed ever closer. I walked on very quiet roads beside a canal and a fast-flowing river, milky-grey with silt from snow melt. Wonderful views made for very enjoyable walking. I was a little tired today and would have liked to take a break, but the Pass and the terrors it posed for former travellers drew me ineluctably on.

St. Maurice to Martigny (27 June)

It was cloudy all day, with a cold wind. There were a few wind turbines where the valley narrowed to funnel and strengthen the wind. What a clever design.

Tomorrow the Via Francigena will leave the Rhône River valley and start to ascend through narrower valleys to Orsières and eventually to the Pass that was often in my mind the closer I got.

There is a train line running all the way from Lausanne to Orsières that pretty much follows the Via Francigena. The train provides flexibility in case of accommodation difficulties or if you don't want to walk a particular stage. There is a potentially tricky section on tomorrow's stage, where the train might be a better option in bad weather.

Martigny to Orsières (Sigeric stop L) (28 June)

There were a few stiff climbs and switchback trails as I traversed the left side of the valley after leaving Martigny, with a couple of steep, scrambling descents requiring care. It was rocky in many places with small jagged boulders to clamber over. The path was often quite narrow, with steep drop-offs, but not alarmingly so. A few places had chains to hold onto. The difficult section took about 80 minutes to cross. Walkers with heavy loads in wet, slippery conditions could find this section tricky to negotiate. Both my guidebooks had warnings about it

After Bouvernier the path seemed to continue into the forest beyond a large land slip but it soon dwindled to faint (probably imaginary) traces as I made my way deeper into the forest. One sometimes sees what one wants to see! My GPS showed the next waypoint was only about 700 metres away and I was heading to it, albeit slowly. So I pressed on through increasingly steep and difficult country, with thick vegetation pulling at my clothes and pack; and steep, crumbly slopes requiring me to haul myself up the sides of loose scree using trees to hang onto. The ground was very broken underfoot with large rocks and fallen branches hidden in dense undergrowth.

At the bottom of the boulder-strewn slope a small river slipped peacefully among mossy stones, dappled with sunlight, unaware of the struggle unfolding in the grim forest above. The river was visible on the left and I could hear the hiss of road traffic in the distance, so I was not worried about getting totally lost, just losing time or getting injured. But the prospect of having to cross the river on slippery rocks and then walk through unknown terrain to reach the road was equally daunting.

After about 45 minutes of strenuous bush-bashing–it seemed like hours–I eventually reached the promised way point and stopped for a snack and to tend assorted nicks from bramble thorns. Apart from feelings of indescribable relief at having reached a known point and safety, I also felt the exhilaration of having overcome a challenge.

Needless to say, I made a poor decision by pressing on into the unknown, especially since I was totally alone. I should have gone back and looked for the correct path around the land slip instead of following the GPS compass. An accident was a real possibility in the rough conditions I struggled through. Or I might have reached a place that actually was impassable and been forced to turn around. A GPS compass may show the way but it does not show the actual walking conditions *en route;* a very important point to remember before one becomes too psychologically committed to pressing on, seduced by the accuracy of a GPS unit.

Orsières to Bourg St. Pierre (Sigeric stop XLIX) (29 June)

It was a steady, relentless climb of 600 metres on a good roads and forested tracks, up the side of the valley all the way to Bourg St. Pierre. It rained all day, getting heavier and colder with increasing altitude. I had a final, hard slog from the valley floor up to Bourg St. Pierre, in rain and sometimes foggy cloud; bleating sheep loomed out of the fog , bunched together to ward off the cold and rain; and cold water dripping steadily down my numb hands and legs.

Where was the village I so desperately wanted to reach? I turned a bend and there it was, with houses looming out of the mist. It was seven degrees Celsius outside, according to the lady who welcomed me at my hotel.

Having arrived early I was able to enjoy both lunch and dinner in the excellent restaurant, served by very friendly staff. Occasionally I looked outside, but cold, damp mist still covered everything and I could see nothing of the views that surrounded me.

Some pilgrims walk the entire distance from Orsières to the Col Grand St. Bernard in one day, a distance of over 25 kilometres. The distance is not the problem; it is the climb of 1600 metres to an altitude of 2400 metres. But doing it all in one day seemed like too much mortification of the flesh for me. I might be a pilgrim in search of salvation, but there is a limit to the amount of suffering I am prepared to accept to achieve it.

Bourg St. Pierre to Col Grand St. Bernard (30 June)

I woke to bright sunshine and a crisp six degrees Celsius. A remarkable change had occurred in the weather overnight. Now I would enjoy sunshine and sublime views for my final assault on the Pass. I set out with waves of exhilaration sweeping over me as glorious mountain vistas unfolded before me. There is majestic beauty in elevated places, well worth the struggle to get there. I wanted to leap and sing!

> *I walk with mindful steps,*
> *embraced by sunlit, snowy peaks.*
> *Flowers smile among rocks.*

I crossed the snow line in mid-morning, in bright sunshine, surrounded by the most enchanting views. Then there were relentless ascents across stony, treeless hillsides. Patches of melting snow grew more frequent as the altitude increased. There were yellow lozenge waymarks for walkers painted on rocks (indicating both directions) all the way across exposed slopes. They would be very welcome if crossing the bleak, hillside in bad weather.

I took the switchback road for the last few kilometres to the Pass to avoid the snow still covering the official path in places. It was a relentless slog in weekend traffic, with noisy, pestilential motorcycles and their anarchic riders roaring past me.

On this side of the Pass, all the streams leaving the mountains eventually flow into the Rhône River, on the other side they flow into the Po River—a river that I would eventually have to cross on my way to Rome, borne across by Danilo the boatman.

The Pass has been in continuous use since the Bronze Age and there are still traces of a Roman road through it. In more unsettled times following the decline of the Roman Empire it was often beset by robbers preying on travellers.

The Great St. Bernard Hospice, located at the highest point of the Pass (2469 Metres), was founded in 1049 to give shelter and safety to distressed travellers. St. Bernard dogs were originally bred as guard dogs for the Hospice, but were found to be excellent rescue dogs as well; the role they are now famous for. Some St. Bernard dogs are still kept at the Hospice to maintain the tradition, and because visitors want to see them.

The Hospice welcomed me as it has done for countless other pilgrims over many centuries. I gratefully accepted the tea offered to me on arrival. I settled into my small room and sank into the spiritual embrace of this place of refuge, thankful for so many undeserved blessings, my trials over.

The dining room was full at dinner. There was only one other pilgrim; the other guests were holiday makers either passing through or trekking in the area. My fellow pilgrim had also met Deborah along the way and had been impressed by her mission to walk the world for love.

As I lay in my bed after dinner before dropping off to sleep, I could hear faint singing coming from somewhere deep in the Hospice. It seemed to seep into every corner, touching everything, entering every room to bless us all and becoming a part of our being; then rising into the sky to be carried on the wind across the mountains, calling to the lost and the bereft that a safe refuge and comfort for the soul awaited them at the Hospice.

I thought of all the countless pilgrims who had slept at peace within these walls. It has been such a privilege to have met so many admirable people; and been inspired by their lives to improve my own life, and by their courage to always seek for something greater while strength remains to me.

Today was such a wonderful day.

Col Grand St. Bernard to Etroubles (1 July)

The weather was wonderfully clear when I woke, so I decided to skip a planned rest day and continue down the mountain to Etroubles. After my cold, foggy arrival at Bourg St. Pierre I was conscious of how quickly the weather can change in mountains, so

one must make the best of good conditions while they
wanted to spend some time with the other guests before
so I had a late breakfast with them and said my goodbyes

Very soon after leaving the Pass I was in Italy. Another country!
Another language! Now I would be able to use the smattering of
Italian I had learned at home. How wonderful it would all be! My
city, Melbourne, is so full of Italian influences, especially in food,
that it almost felt like I was coming home.

The lake at the Pass was still frozen and there was still a lot of
snow on the Italian side of the mountains, so I took the road for a
while. Later, I had to cross hard packed snow at times. There was
even one dedicated cross-country skier making the most of the last
disappearing snow of winter.

The route was very picturesque below the snow line. But parts of
the path after St. Rhemy (Sigeric stop XLVIII) were quite
unpleasant; very narrow in places, with steepish descents and
crumbly edges hidden in grass. Perfect for a stumble and fall if I
relaxed my vigilance.

The 1100 metre descent to Etroubles was not as easy as I had
expected. Different muscles are stressed during long descents.

Etroubles to Aosta (Sigeric stop XLVII) (2 July)

Much of the day was a muscle-busting descent of 700m on good,
but steep, paths–especially after Gignod. It started with a climb out
of Etroubles, then a very nice walk in forest beside a tranquil water
channel before the long descent into Aosta. The day got steadily
warmer with lower altitude. Small orchards started to appear in the
warmer climate.

I decided to have a rest day in Aosta. The walk seemed to have
become more of a chore after crossing the Pass and leaving the
Hospice. I was feeling flat and demotivated. What was the point of
all this struggle?

Aosta (3 July)

I was alarmed to discover that all the navigation data I needed for
after Aosta had disappeared from my GPS unit. I had similar
problems before setting out from Besançon, but I was able to get
replacement data emailed to me, which I loaded into my GPS unit at
a local internet café. Something must have gone wrong with the
upload process, but it was not evident to me at the time. The GPS

unit could still record my actual track and I could still use it as a compass, so why worry? I had an excellent guide book as backup.

Aosta is the first large city pilgrims reach after crossing the Pass. It has been settled since time immemorial and was a major Roman city. The location, at the confluence of two rivers and commanding the approaches to the Pass, made Aosta strategically important. That also meant the city was frequently invaded during and after the decline of the Roman Empire. Many historical ruins, including a Roman theatre, still exist.

Aosta to Chatillon (4 July)

Today was a difficult day, quite hot, with many short but steep ascents and descents on minor roads and tracks shadowing the two main roads to Aosta; the *autostrada* and the older SS26. It would have been possible to avoid the strenuous hillside paths by following the easier and shorter SS26 all the way to Chatillon.

The Via Francigena route was generally well waymarked, but care was needed just before the waterfall of Rus Chandianaz, which was dry when I passed. Then there was an interminable but shady walk along a good path across a hillside, with a water channel on one side of the path, cooling the air.

Shortly before Chatillon there is a derelict hamlet which the Via Francigena bypasses. But the track was hidden in thick grass (not much foot traffic was evident) and I entered the hamlet by mistake, having to clamber over large rocks and fallen building debris to get back to the Via Francigena.

But it was an interesting diversion. Why were all those strong stone houses just abandoned and allowed to fall into ruins? At such times one is conscious of the implacable march of history. Our lives are so short, historically speaking, that we are unaware of the great historical currents that are shaping the world. Only many years later, when we, or our descendants, look back, will we be able to see the times through which we lived in their true historical perspective. What seems important today may turn out to be an historical side track. Other forces might overwhelm us, and new, unexpected discoveries might radically alter our future lives.

It seemed like I would never get to Chatillon, but eventually I arrived, drenched in sweat, extremely tired, and found a small, but welcome, room at the Albergo Dufour.

There was no accommodation available for tomorrow at Issogne when I called ahead to book. The owner of the Albergo was very helpful in finding me a place to stay off the Via Francigena at Verres,

48

including printing maps and showing me the route in Google Street View. If the entire Via Francigena was available in Street View, we would never have to walk it. We could sit at our ease in front of our computer, with drinks and snacks to hand, and let Street View show us the way. Perhaps one day we will be able to don virtual reality goggles and do the same thing, living our lives in the computer, never leaving the house!

Chatillon to Verres (5 July)

There were good "Route 103" waymarks today, so I decided to follow them, and not my guidebook, to Montjovet (Sigeric stop XLVI), hoping I was not embarking on a long, grand tour of the district. It turned out to be an enjoyable walk. Then there was a long, boring walk along the road beside the river Dora Baltea to Verres.

I stayed at the Ostello Il Casello next to the train station. There were no shops or places to eat close by and I did not want to walk into the centre of Verres to get a good meal. The lady in charge of the Ostello cooked dinner for me, the solitary guest, while she and her two young children ate at a nearby table, engrossed in their computers. Another guest clattered into their room late in the night, waking me from a deep sleep. At least it was not a pestilential tour group.

Verres to Pont Saint Martin (6 July)

I was well out of the mountains now. The hills were losing their sharp edges and the valleys were opening up into flat farmland. Sometimes I would look back up the valley and see, far away, almost out of sight, the snowy tips of mountains through which I had walked a few days ago.

There was a sense of wistfulness in looking back, of something precious that had been lost in the fading past; and a longing to be once more among flowery mountain meadows and placid lakes, where the spirit could soar again and be at peace: another chance to seek forgiveness and perhaps to find the path I might have taken all those years ago.

> *"The Moving Finger writes; and, having writ,*
> *Moves on: nor all thy Piety nor Wit*
> *Shall lure it back to cancel half a Line,*
> *Nor all thy Tears wash out a Word of it."*

(Edward Fitzgerald's translation of The Rubáiyát of Omar Khayyam, 1859).

Sadly and regretfully, I turned aside from such reveries and lifted my eyes to the hills before me, resuming a physical and a spiritual journey still to be completed. A journey that, deep in my heart, I knew would never be completed.

Vineyards appeared today for the first time since leaving Lausanne on the far side of the Alps. The grapes were about the size of a small pea and would soon swell into luscious fruit in the summer sun. The harvest would be at hand for another year when summer waned and autumn approached.

An impressive feature of today's walk was the huge fortress of Bard dating back to the 4th century and dominating the busy tourist town of Hone. It was another fortress commanding the strategic Alpine routes from France to Italy. The present 19th century structure is a good example of military architecture of the period. It could accommodate several hundred soldiers with all the supplies necessary to resist a siege of a few months.

Pont St. Martin was very picturesque with its Roman Bridge forming the centrepiece of the town. Actually, the restored "Roman Bridge" was a bit like grandpa's axe that has had five new handles and three new heads. I walked over the hog-back bridge, surprised by how steep the actual roadway was.

I stayed at B&B il Castel. It was very central and close to the Roman Bridge. The inviting flower-covered building raised my spirits as soon as I saw it. They rose further on meeting the owner and being shown to my room.

I was served an excellent early breakfast next morning. The owner is an experienced hiker and he tried to restore my GPS data, but to no avail. This B&B was another of my favourite stays so far in Italy.

Pont Saint Martin to Ivrea (Sigeric stop XLV) (7 July)

There were very good Via Francigena signs in a large "street sign" format on this stage, so I simply followed them instead of paying too much attention to my guidebook.

I took a diversion to see a small lake, Lago Pistono, near Montalto Dora. The shore was crowded with walkers and families having Sunday picnics. I was a little unsure of my onward route and asked how far it was to the place I planned to stay the night. Smiling faces assured me that it was very close, virtually just around the next bend. I could be there in an instant. My spirits rose at this gratifying news, but sank just as quickly when I realised that all the smiling faces had driven here in their cars and were giving me a driver's perspective on time. But I thanked them nevertheless and back-tracked until I found a known point and was confident of the way forward. No more bashing on regardless! I had learnt that lesson when walking from Martigny to Orsières.

Ivrea, my final destination today, was very busy with people attending the annual Festival of St. Savino, the patron saint of Ivrea, starting on July 7 each year. During the festival a horse fair also takes place, with carriage exhibitions and horse shows on the main square. The Festival was in full swing when I arrived. All the cafés were full of people having a great time, exuding goodwill to all. Ivrea also celebrates the Carnival Festival in February with its famous Battle of the Oranges, a spectacular event that attracts thousands of visitors. It would be interesting to attend that festival—if you care to walk the Via Francigena in winter.

Ivrea to Roppolo (8 July)

Much of the route today was on excellent tracks through forest, and fields of wheat and corn; with a final lovely walk to Roppolo beside trellised kiwi fruit vines overlooking Lago di Viverone.

I stayed at Villa Emilia, the warmest and most enjoyable place to stay on my whole journey from Besançon to Vercelli. One other pilgrim was staying there and we had a very pleasant time. I felt very much at home. My room and bed were comfortable. Having a comfortable bed had become a major preoccupation for me after having slept in so many beds which either sank precipitously in the middle or threatened to toss me out every time I rolled over.

There was a nice garden and a separate open building for meals and relaxation. After doing our daily chores, we whiled away the afternoon chatting and playing with Loretta's friendly little dog.

Loretta (the owner) had lived in Pakistan and Egypt and the whole place was decorated with things she had brought back. It turned out that we had both been to the same remote places in both countries; Siwa in Egypt and the Hunza Valley in Pakistan. The local shops were closed and Loretta insisted on cooking a full, gut-busting Italian dinner for us.

Good people like Loretta deserve support. They face plenty of pressure to drive down their prices, as well as bureaucratic controls on what they can and can't do. Low prices might be justified for a really basic B&B or *albergo*, but not for people like Loretta who go

51

out of their way to make pilgrims welcome and comfortable in their homes.

Roppolo to San Germano (9 July)

Loretta prepared a filling breakfast for us and made a booking for our stay tonight at San Germano. The weather started cloudy with thunder and light rain for a couple of hours.

After Santhia (Sigeric stop XLIV) we walked through very flat farmland, nearly all rice fields. The Via Francigena wound its way among them on narrow roads separating the water-filled fields. We could have simply walked down the busy main road from Santhia to San Germano to save distance and time. But why risk life and limb and be stressed on a road when one could walk at peace through tranquil farmland?

There was only one day to go for me this year, but my companion would continue to Rome, hoping to arrive on August 14. I felt very strong now and wished I could continue to Rome myself, step by step, one day at a time.

San Germano to Vercelli (Sigeric stop XLIII) (10 July)

We followed the busy main road until we were able to take a side track into the rice fields like we did yesterday, where it was very pleasant walking in excellent weather, without the noise of traffic. Not all the rice field paths were straightforward. In one place we threw our packs over a small irrigation channel and jumped across, rather than waste time looking for another way round among the fields. Later, near Vercelli, the path was blocked by a fence and we had to backtrack a few hundred metres and walk on the main road for the final stretch into Vercelli.

My journey to Vercelli ended as it had begun weeks ago with Deborah at Besançon; in the company of another pilgrim whose journey to Rome would take many more days. Deborah was somewhere ahead of me, spreading her message of love as a transforming power in our troubled world. Herman, my companion of the last two days, arrived safely in Rome on August 13 and would soon return to his family in The Netherlands.

I will return to Vercelli in 2014, when winter has passed and spring has burst forth, and set out anew on the final leg of the ancient road to Rome.

o o o

Photographs

Photo 1: The Via Francigena passing through the Alps soon after leaving Bourg St. Pierre.

Photo 2: A beautiful view from vineyards looking across Lake Geneva to the mountains, after Lausanne.

Photo 3: The lavish interior of the church at the Col Great St. Bernard. Many small towns in Italy have surprisingly lavish interiors which are occasionally exuberantly Baroque.

Vercelli to Rome

2014

Now that I had crossed the Swiss Alps it seemed that all the difficult walking had been done. Accommodation was much easier to find in Italy. The Via Francigena was better known in Italy than in other countries. My equipment was all sorted and worked well. I had developed an efficient daily routine for all the essential chores which had to be done every day.

All these optimistic thoughts made me almost believe, or at least made me hope, that the final section down the leg of Italy would be a formality. I had simply to put one foot in front of the other and stay healthy and I would be in Rome before I knew it.

Vercelli to Robbio (15 June)

I set out at 7:30 am in light rain that got steadily heavier as the morning progressed. Rain is good–you can test your poncho! But it was also good to find dry shelter for a snack under a road overpass. The path was flat, through irrigated rice fields, often on high embankments, wide enough to take vehicles, separating the fields.

Today was only a short stage. It was my first day back on the Via Francigena for a year, so I did not want to walk too far. I reached Robbio by noon and had lunch chatting about my long walk with some very interested locals. I decided to stay in Robbio instead of continuing to Mortara, and then spent ages finding my bed for the night.

It was Sunday and the Municipal Office which had arranged a bed for me was closed, so I had no way of finding where I was to sleep that night. None of the locals was able to help me because the accommodation was not a regular B&B or hostel that everyone would know about in such a small town. In desperation I asked the local *carabinieri*. The officer made a few phone calls and showed me my room–behind the Municipal Centre which I had stood in front of an hour before.

I felt very tired despite the short walk. I need a week on the road to adjust and become fully conditioned. Short stages for the first couple of days seemed to help.

The booming bell above my room was thankfully silent during the night. But in the distance I could occasionally hear a very musical church bell with a pure, clear, almost feminine sound that comforted me through the long night.

Robbio to Mortara (16 June)

The rain had stopped in the night and it was cool and cloudy when I set out. This part of Italy is a large rice-growing area and the Via Francigena passed through more irrigated fields of rice. Route signage was very good today, so I hardly needed to navigate. I just followed the signs.

Via Francigena signs come in great variety. Probably the most common are small red/white stickers wrapped around light poles or stuck on walls. There are also large official "street signs" that come in three varieties: one for walkers, another for cyclists and a third for drivers. Then there are numerous informal signs and arrows painted on trees, roadside crash barriers and even on the tarmac itself.

I had settled into my daily routine and was feeling more relaxed today. The pilgrimage drug was starting to kick in again.

I stayed at the Hotel della Torre, with a nice room and comfortable bed. It was above a busy restaurant, but thankfully there was no noise at night. The big disadvantage of staying in hotels is that I very rarely met any other pilgrims. That had been the case ever since I left Canterbury, but I hoped it would change in Italy, where the Via Francigena is better known.

Mortara to Bozzolo (17 June)

I slept very well last night and was on the road at 6:30 am in cool cloudy weather that turned into light rain as I arrived at Bozzolo. I had decided to take a detour to visit Bozzolo, instead of taking the usual Via Francigena route via Garlasco.

There were quite a few birds on the rice fields, mainly herons and egrets looking for frogs and fish. I often saw ripples at the edges of irrigation channels as I passed, presumably frogs thinking I was a giant heron and making a timely escape. A couple of rabbits hopped into the bushes ahead of me, no doubt kept in control by the beautiful, sleek ferrets I saw much later on the pilgrimage. Many small, very beautiful, iridescent green beetles lay dead on the shadier paths. Why? A few plum trees grew beside the path in one spot, but they were not quite ripe yet. Edible, but very tart. In a couple of weeks I should be able to feast on them.

The Santuario Madonna della Bozzola has a beautiful church with a lavish interior, set in tranquil surroundings. My accommodation at the Albergo Margherita was right next to the Santuario.

The Santuario was founded in 1465, after a thirteen-year-old, deaf and dumb girl had a vision in a storm, in which the Virgin Mary told her that she wanted a sanctuary built here. The girl's hearing and speech were miraculously restored and she returned home to tell the villagers about her vision. The Santuario still has a vibrant spiritual and cultural life today. It also runs a recovery centre for young people with addictions. That is a good way for the Church to stay in tune with local social needs, and be relevant to its communities. I saw other positive examples later on my pilgrimage.

I met a group of Sicilians at dinner who were working on a project at a factory in the area, and were intrigued that anyone would want to walk to Rome. "Rome!" they cried dismissively. "If you want to walk, come to Sicily!"

Bozzolo to Pavia (Sigeric stop XLI) (18 June)

I started walking early, in cool, cloudy weather that gradually turned into a warm, sunny day. Flat, irrigated rice fields were slowly giving way to slightly hillier terrain, but the gradients were very gentle, not like those to come in the next week or so. It had just dawned on me that the mountains had not finished with the Alps–I would have to cross the Apennine Mountains as well.

Blackberries were starting to ripen and soon would be very edible. It is easy to recognise fruits like plums and blackberries by the wayside, but it would be nice to be able to identify other edible plants along the paths I walked. Much of the wayside vegetation was very lush and I am sure it included salad greens and other plants that would have made a very welcome addition to my *en route* snacks and meals. I wondered if there was a smartphone app for identifying such plants. It would be great to be able to take a photo of a plant and have an app identify it on the spot. Mushrooms are a different matter; one must really know mushrooms before eating any wild ones.

The last kilometre or so to Pavia was very enjoyable, on forest paths next to the wide Ticino River, with enticing views across the water to the city. It is a popular spot among the locals and several joggers and walkers stopped me for a chat. There was a sandy 'beach' close to Pavia, complete with swimmers and sunbathers.

Probably the most eye-catching structure pilgrims see as they enter Pavia is the *Ponte Coperto*, or *Ponte Vecchio*, the Covered

Bridge. The old bridge, dating from the 14th century was heavily damaged in World War Two and collapsed further two years later. Construction of the present bridge began in 1949. Like the old bridge, it has a chapel.

I stayed at the Hotel Aurora and was able to get an excellent early breakfast next morning, including yoghurt, juice, cheese and cold meats. Many places I stayed at provided only bread (or cakes) with jam, plus coffee. A good breakfast always made a very motivating start to the day.

Pavia to Santa Cristina (Sigeric stop XL) (19 June)

I set out at 07:30 am in clear, warm weather that grew hot as the day progressed. The early morning walk out of Pavia was lovely, along the Ticino River, past the beautiful Covered Bridge, its bricks glowing red and gold in the early sunlight. Later on the day became very hot, and it was very unpleasant walking on roads among cornfields into Santa Cristina. The high corn closely lining the road stifled any breeze and seemed to concentrate the heat.

My dormitory accommodation was provided by the Parrocchia di Sta. Cristina e Bissone. I had a comfortable bunk and even disposable sheets and pillowcases. That was a first, and a welcome change from bedding that had seen too many pilgrims, especially pillows that exuded the sour smell of stale sweat. I could buy drinks and snacks in the busy church hall below the dormitory. Perfect!

There was a very vibrant atmosphere in the church hall, which seems to be the town meeting place. Older men were noisily playing cards, with their wives watchfully second-guessing them from the sidelines. Teenage boys and girls were hanging out and pretending to ignore each other. The priest was bustling about keeping an eye on everything. I sat blissfully amongst them, eating my snack, completely ignored, just immersed in the normal life of this small community.

There were two other pilgrims staying here, an older French woman who had walked from Paris and a German girl who had started in Lausanne. Both were *en route* to Rome. We had a good pilgrim dinner in the bar opposite the church, with a discount for showing our pilgrim passports.

I was beginning to find that the Via Francigena and pilgrimage were better known and appreciated in Italy than in either France or Switzerland. This impression was amply borne out by my experiences here and later on.

The Catholic faith seemed to be more overt in Italy than in the other countries I had crossed. Many small towns have churches with surprisingly lavish interiors, even the one here, in this small town. Some decay was evident, but nothing like the dilapidation of many other emptying churches in more secular countries. One passes many small wayside shrines and statues.

Many Western countries have become increasingly secular. While I welcome the freedom from imposed dogma that comes with secularism, I also recognise that faith, and its manifestation in many forms of religion, has an important place as a guide to personal conduct and in our relations with other people; as well as a solace in time of grief and difficulty. A strong spiritual belief seems to be an important factor among hostages and those who have survived privations and torture in prisoner of war camps.

Faith is not rational in a scientific sense. If it were it would not be faith. But that does not detract from its place in the world. The particular form of faith that an individual has is largely irrelevant in a spiritual sense, although it might be very important to misguided people who want to impose conformity with doctrinal specifics on others.

Science and logic on the other hand seek to explain the world that we experience and contemplate. Science is utilitarian, because it enables us to make useful predictions about the future and to build new things based on its theories. Science and engineering keep a plane in the sky, but faith may be of immense comfort to passengers when the engines fail.

Both religion and science have their place. All the difficulties arise when one intrudes on the other and seeks to impose its will on everything as the only path to "truth". One can never disprove faith with logic.

Santa Cristina to Orio Litta (20 June)

Today was a short stage before catching Danilo's ferry across the Po tomorrow. Pilgrims need to book the day before. Danilo was reluctant to make the trip for only one pilgrim at a time (fuel for his fast boat costs money), so the three of us from Santa Cristina agreed to cross together.

Readers familiar with Greek mythology will be aware of Charon ferrying the dead across the River Styx. Danilo is not like that. Quite the opposite!

The man in charge of the accommodation at Orio Litta, the Cascina San Pietro, dropped by in the afternoon to see how we were settling in and made ferry bookings with Danilo for next day. He also showed us a good pizzeria for dinner, with a television playing an important football game from the World Cup, which had the staff totally transfixed.

Orio Litta to Crossing the Po River to Piacenza (Sigeric stop XXXVIII) (21 June)

Today was all about Danilo and crossing the Po River. We arrived about 9 am and Danilo arrived in his fast boat shortly after, as arranged. The crossing itself took about twenty minutes. Sometimes the actual landing spot changes depending on the river level or if any flood damage has occurred.

Then we gathered round Danilo's great record book in his garden to pore over old entries and marvel at so much dedication over so many years. He also has a chart going back to 1998 showing the numbers and nationalities of pilgrims and where they were going to. There were 2340 people recorded on the chart, with 379 crossing in 2013. Not all pilgrims take the ferry, as there is an alternate, but longer, road route.

It was quite moving to be a part of Danilo's small signing ceremony and to be a link with those who have gone before us, far back to Sigeric's day, and those who will follow us, who knows how far into the future. I hope future pilgrims will be able to see Danilo's great book and its dedicated entries, long after we have all passed away. To touch a name written by hand on real paper in the distant past is to make a connection with that person and to wonder who they were, what brought them to this tranquil spot on the great river and how their lives unfolded.

Danilo plays an important part in the cultural life of the Via Francigena. It is all very well to spend money on signage and route improvements and nice brochures; but I hope that people who help to bring the Via Francigena alive are also recognised in some tangible way. If they ever build a new bridge near here, I hope it is called Danilo Bridge. Pilgrimage is a human endeavour for those who undertake it, aided by quiet and humble people who ease their journey.

Piacenza to Fiorenzuola d'Arda (Sigeric stop XXXVII) (22 June)

I was on the road at 7 am in cool weather, but the day warmed up quickly. The recommended route has a long section winding through fields, adding extra distance to the stage. I bypassed that section by walking down the main road. It had wide, safe verges and the Sunday morning traffic was light. On other stages paths were being upgraded parallel to main roads with barriers separating walkers from the traffic, so that walkers could save distance while walking in safety. It is an excellent initiative that I hope will be extended where road conditions and funding allow.

Some of the smaller country roads can be more dangerous than main roads because a walker could be hidden by bends, and drivers might be chatting on their phones, not expecting to see anyone walking on the road. That happened to me a few times on the Via Francigena. So when facing oncoming traffic I tried to see if the driver had a phone glued to his (or her) ear.

I had to ford two streams today, but the water level was low and a ferryman like Danilo was not required.

I slept at accommodation provided by the Parrocchia di San Fiorenzo, but the room was uncomfortably small for the three of us who shared it. I moved my mattress downstairs and slept on the floor in the common area.

Fiorenzuola d'Arda to Fidenza (Sigeric stop XXXVI) (23 June)

Rice fields have given way to lucerne, corn and other crops. Hay was being cut and raked into long lines to dry in the warm, sunny weather. A giant machine slowly munched its way down a line of raked hay. Hay disappeared into the front end and emerged at the rear as big, plastic-wrapped cylinders that regularly plopped onto the ground as the monster advanced.

I had a break at the wonderful Abbey of Chiaravalle della Columba, founded after a visit by St. Bernard of Clairvaux to Piacenza in 1135. It is a Cistercian abbey, and a great contrast to the decaying complex at Clairvaux which I visited in 2012. It is a quiet, beautiful spot, with a hotel on the site that would make a restful stop if you could arrange your walking stages to suit. There is a café just outside the Abbey, so you won't starve.

The whole length of the nave was laid with a flower tapestry for Corpus Christi. It was breathtakingly beautiful, with the smells of the flowers still in the air.

The cloister has remarkable "knotted" corner columns supporting the roof of the colonnade surrounding the central garden. It was as if someone had taken each column and knotted it like a piece of cord.

Was the master mason just showing off his skills, or was it some Cistercian symbolism?

I spent the night at the Convento di San Francesco, set in very tranquil surroundings, but some distance out of town—as were all the San Francesco convents I stayed at. There was a café next door with WiFi and very friendly staff. Lots of young people were coming and going; the boys were either playing soccer across the street to impress watching girls, or just hanging out at the café.

I really liked the Convento and its setting. It was restful and rejuvenating—as good as taking a day off from walking.

Fidenza to Medesano (Sigeric stop XXXV) (24 June)

Today was the first day of climbing since leaving the rice fields; with quite a long uphill slog shortly after leaving Fidenza and again after Costamezzana. The country was getting hillier as I approached the Cisa Pass dividing the Ligurian and Tuscan Apennines. There was nowhere to have breakfast when I left Fidenza, so when I found a tree with ripe plums my spirits immediately rose. I could have a balanced diet if only I knew which of the luxuriant roadside weeds I could safely eat.

I had a very relaxing stop for a late breakfast at Trattororia Lo Scoiattolo at Costamezzana. The pilgrim-friendly owner has a big visitor's book to sign. It reminded me of Danilo again. If you ever go there, look for number 256. That's me! Classical music was playing— a Vivaldi violin concerto. Wonderful home-made cake was available. Two big wedges were hardly enough.

No one answered the phone when I tried to book church accommodation at Medesano. I went to the church a couple of times after I arrived, but no one was there and the accommodation was locked. So I opted for a hotel recommended by a local in the café where I had lunch. He had heard my unsuccessful phone calls and introduced himself.

The owner called a friend to come to the café when she learned that I was from Australia. The friend has a daughter working in Australia whom she missed, and I was a link to Australia that she could talk to and somehow feel a little closer to her distant daughter.

I felt very tired and a little down after arriving today. Sitting alone in an empty hotel did not help. The streets were baking hot and empty, so I had little incentive to wander about outside. A few minor aches and pains had developed on the climbs today. Ah well, pilgrimage is not meant to be easy!

63

Tomorrow I will face the first long slog up to the Cisa Pass. Italy is all downhill if you see it on a map, the way a human leg points down. How can there be climbs and passes??

Medesano to Cassio (25 June)

There was a stiff climb out of Medesano followed by a couple of brutal descents to test the thigh muscles. Then, after Fornovo di Taro, it was a steady climb most of the way to Cassio.

The day was cool and became overcast, with thunder later and brief periods of light rain. At higher altitudes I passed into mist and poor visibility. I caught up with a cyclist with large panniers on the front and rear of his bike, and a guitar strapped to his back. The road was so steep he had to weave back and forth across it with his heavy load. I went past him and he disappeared behind me into the mist.

But the mist rose eventually to reveal beautiful mountain vistas. It was like someone had gradually drawn aside a gigantic curtain that had concealed the landscape.

Oak trees and conifers became more common as the altitude increased. I saw lots of small wildflowers along the route: pink, yellow, blue; with an occasional fragrant smell wafted on the air.

Years ago on a pilgrimage to Santiago I met a German pilgrim gazing wistfully at some small blue flowers by the roadside. He explained the significance to him of *die Blaue Blume*. "In German literature *die Blaue Blume* symbolizes inspiration, love; and striving for the unreachable. It symbolizes hope and the beauty of things." Such feelings often came over me at inspiring or beautiful places on my long walks; they were part of the essence of pilgrimage for me.

Flowers, however beautiful, are not always edible, alas. I came upon more plum trees later; and also figs, but they were small and quite unripe. Vines were starting to appear, with roses planted at the ends of the rows. The grapes were still very tiny. A small deer (edible) bounded away from me into the trees. It knew I was not St. Francis, but I would never hurt such a beautiful creature.

Today was wonderfully exhilarating and I felt strong and refreshed by the mountains. My spirits rose even further when I reached the Ostello at Cassio and a warm welcome—and another familiar pilgrim who had crossed the Po River with me.

Cassio to Ostello della Cisa (26 June)

The walk to Berceto (Sigeric stop XXXIII) was very beautiful, on undulating paths through fields with scenic views across valleys to the mountains. I passed through picturesque stone villages with narrow streets and bright flowers decorating doors and windows. Rain started just before I reached Berceto, and I hurried as quickly as I could down the slippery path, hoping to escape the worst of the downpour. I stopped for a welcome coffee with another pilgrim in a packed café; but the rain did not ease up.

My companion had decided to stay the night here, so I pressed on alone to the Ostello della Cisa, 1100 metres above sea level. The route after Berceto was relentlessly uphill for most of the day, sometimes on rough, stony paths.

The *Ostello* was empty and locked when I arrived. There is no village here, just a few other locked buildings. A cold, light rain–Scottish mist–was falling. Four pm came and went. I was still the only person around. My host had booked a bed for me the night before, but what if something had gone wrong and no one arrived to let me in? There was no phone reception, so I could not even call for help.

I investigated the other buildings and found an open shed for storing firewood. It was cramped, but I resolved to sleep there if necessary. That prospect seemed less desirable as I sat in the shed out of the rain and noticed a small tick crawling up my boot. Then there was another.

But the lady in charge arrived in the midst of these gloomy thoughts and all was well. She cooked me a full Italian meal and left out the makings of hearty breakfast before going home. I was the only person staying in the *Ostello*. I relaxed in the large sitting area, drinking tea, and poring over its collection of books and maps. All I could see through the window were trees on the far side of the empty road. It was as if I were alone in a sanctuary, safe from the elements and prowling wolves.

Ostello della Cisa to Pontremoli (Sigeric stop XXXI) (27 June)

I decided to take an alternate route along the road today to avoid having to retrace my steps and slog uphill to re-join the main Via Francigena path which wound through hilly country. The Ostello della Cisa is not on the main Via Francigena route and you have to descend quite a bit to reach it.

I crossed the "official" Ciso Pass on the main road before the souvenir shop had opened, so I was unable to get a stamp for my pilgrim passport. There is also a substantial church at the pass, but it was also closed at that hour. The Ciso Pass seemed a bit mundane after the Col Grand St. Bernard.

After the pass, the walk was mostly on quiet minor roads with picturesque views and some long descents. It was another very enjoyable walk, with a quiet, comfortable room at the Convento Cappuccini to wrap up the day.

Pontremoli to Aulla (Sigeric stop XXX) (28 June)

I took the Via Francigena cycle route from Villafranca to Aulla to save some distance. The main route for walkers takes a meandering wander through fields to avoid busy roads, but adding at unwanted extra distance to the stage.

The route I took demonstrated the safety problems walkers face on many main roads and is probably why the official Via Francigena route often avoids them. There was no verge and dense vegetation came right up to the tarmac. Walkers have no choice but to walk on the tarmac. And in this case a crash barrier (slightly dented from a previous collision!) prevents a walker from pushing into the vegetation to avoid oncoming vehicles. It would take just one distracted driver blabbing or texting on his or her phone to wipe you out.

The accommodation at the Abbazia di San Caprasio was quite full when I arrived, but I was able to get a bed. There was a large group of American students walking some of the highlights of the Via Francigena. A teacher was in charge of the group and they also had an Italian guide or 'tour director' to navigate and handle all the administrative details. All the students had to do was walk. They must have had a tough time of it because the bathroom rubbish bins were full with used bandaids, compeed, and the discarded wrappings of other first aid items. But they were polite and quiet; possibly their tiring walk had taken some of the exuberance out of them.

I liked the accommodation. Pilgrims were greeted in a friendly, efficient way and offered a cup of coffee. It was very organised and business-like. I was told I could get an excellent pilgrim dinner in a restaurant just across the bridge.

The Abbey of San Caprasio was founded in the 8th century, and its museum and displays form one of the main attractions in Aulla. The historic centre of the town was destroyed by bombing in World

War Two. The centre has long been rebuilt, but, like most post-war reconstruction in Europe, the new architecture has a distinctive 1950's style.

Aulla to Sarzana (29 June)

I had a brutal climb out of Aulla on narrow, steep, rocky paths often overgrown with thorny brambles and I was thankful to be wearing a long-sleeved shirt and long pants. One has to be very careful that brambles don't snag your eyes as you push past. A few times on the Via Francigena I have had my hat snatched off by overhanging brambles. In ancient times people often believed that mischievous demons caused such minor mishaps.

The day began cool with misty tendrils of foggy cloud draping the hills and valleys. Compact hilltop villages poked above the cloud, the stone houses huddling together to ward off winter chills–and, in earlier times, invaders.

After about an hour of climbing there was a welcome rest area with sheltered seats and a table. Then I had to negotiate a short, steep descent on uncomfortable paths to Old Vechietto, followed by another rugged ascent. But it was all over in several hours–apart from the final long, steep descent into Sarzana. The stage was short and well waymarked, but the gradients and rocks made it difficult in places.

A friendly dog appeared out of nowhere in the forest and followed me silently and companionably for quite a while, then wandered off into the trees. It got me thinking. Wolves are making a tentative comeback in Europe, and in Italy there are estimated to be about 600 wolves roaming about the remoter forests. That's something to think about as you pitch your tent for the night. But I suppose wolves were a more real threat in Sigeric's day.

The climate and vegetation were also quite different in the 10th century. Extensive forests were cleared for farms and to provide charcoal and wood to fuel the beginnings of industrialisation. A few remnants do remain. In France I passed a protected remnant of ancient forest. Today, when you walk through a forest along the Via Francigena, all the trees are young, a few decades old at most. All the large, ancient trees were cut down long ago.

A surprising variety of crops grew in this small area: olives, grapes, peaches and lemons. Chestnut trees grew in the forest. Cicadas were singing as the day warmed up.

I stayed the night in the B&B La Locanda dei Limone to avoid having to compete with the big student group for a bed. It was very tranquil, and had a central courtyard planted with lemons, peaches, grapes and small tart kumquats.

There was a wide veranda with table and chairs outside the rooms for relaxing and eating. It made a nice shelter when an afternoon storm struck. I sat there writing my notes and laughed at it. "You can't hurt me, Storm," I exulted silently as the rain poured off the roof.

Sarzana to Massa (30 June)

I walked with two other pilgrims, occasional companions from previous days, until our ways parted. They took the main route to Massa through the hills and vineyards, and I took the alternate route by the sea. It added about four kilometres to the stage but I yearned to see the ocean and to have a symbolic foot-washing in its waters.

It was a disappointment, not like the wonderful walk along the shore of Lake Geneva that I had hoped for. Most of the route to Marina di Massa was along a cycle path next to the main road, some distance from the beach. I saw only occasional sparkling glimpses of the ocean.

Most of the shore was taken up by private property or commercial buildings and there was no convenient way to walk down to the beach to dip a toe in the water. It always bugs me when ordinary citizens are prevented by those more privileged from enjoying free access to good beaches.

At length I turned away from the sea for the long uphill walk along shady streets to Massa itself.

White scars on the mountains looked like snow from a distance, but they were marble quarries. A road sign earlier in the day pointed to Carrara, a very famous quarry that has been worked since Roman times. The famous statue of David was sculpted from a block of Carrara marble. Some of the street gutters in the Massa area are also edged in marble–at the opposite end of the aesthetic scale.

The serried ranks of the Apennine Mountains, with their soft shades of grey in early morning light, were behind me now. My route will turn inland, away from the mountains and the whispering sea. Rome still seemed so far away.

I was given a mattress on the floor at the Convento Cappuccini. Two pilgrims I had met previously had arrived earlier and had been given the only room available for pilgrim accommodation. They pressed comforts on me to make it more comfortable to sleep on the floor, but it was not necessary because one of the monks returned with a foldup stretcher. The Convento is beautifully located, overlooking the town, but there is no food or shops in the vicinity. We had to walk down the hill to the town to eat and it was quite a climb back to the Convento on full stomachs.

Massa to Camaiore (Sigeric stop XXVII) (1 July)

After a stiff climb out of Massa the walk was very enjoyable, on quiet roads, through vineyards, with occasional glimpses of the ocean. But it was not as spectacular as some of the vineyard walks overlooking Lake Geneva earlier on the Via Francigena.

My companions and I struck the mother lode of plum trees! Their branches were drooping under the heavy weight of sweet, juicy, perfectly ripe plums. The low-hanging fruit were soon devoured, and a walking pole was usefully employed on the higher branches. What a feast!

The streets of Pietrasanta are full of attention-grabbing art works. The Colombian artist and sculptor Fernando Botero visits Pietrasanta for part of the year. One of his corpulent bronze sculptures is located at the entrance to the town. Quirky restaurants, unusual shops and art galleries abound.

Pietrasanta grew to importance during the 15th century, mainly due to its connection with marble. Michelangelo was the first sculptor to recognize the beauty of the local stone. Quarries in the region are still active and Via Francigena passes several factories processing large blocks of marble.

The plan was to have a rest day, and be a tourist, in Lucca tomorrow, so I have booked a hotel there. I don't really like hotels after all my stays in religious and communal lodgings. Italy really excels in that respect, unlike other countries on the Via Francigena, where it was often inconvenient to arrange parish accommodation– at least in my experience.

Hotels are so isolating. Family-run B&Bs along the Via Francigena are usually preferable, because their owners are often listed in pilgrim guidebooks, so they know about the Via Francigena and are often interested in pilgrims. Some have even walked the same routes themselves.

The accommodation at the Oratorio il Colosseo in Camaiore was conveniently located just outside the centre of town, with numerous cafes and shops close by.

I met another pilgrim who was interested in Buddhism and was on her way to stay at a Buddhist Retreat. We discussed some aspects of Buddhism that I find particularly appealing. All things change and we should not get too attached to material things. Respect all life. Walk with mindful steps, fully conscious of all about you; or, more simplistically, live in the moment.

She suggested we might like to go to the Retreat together. I was greatly tempted, although it would have meant abandoning my pilgrimage to Rome. But perhaps the goal I had set myself was not the one I should be striving for. Who knows? In life we come to many forks and must choose one path or the other; with little to guide our choice except the hope of a more fulfilling future.

The two of us had dinner at the Ristorante l'Angolo del Gusti on the Piazza XXIX Maggio. They make fantastic gourmet *panini*. The staff were friendly and helpful. It was a wonderful meal, topped off by some excellent fruit we bought on the way back to our rooms.

Camaiore to Lucca (Sigeric stop XXVI) (2 July)

I found more ripe plums along the side of the path. Of course I could always get the most wonderful fruit in shops without foraging in the wild. It was all so fresh and ready to eat–not like the rocky stone fruit inflicted on shoppers in my supermarket at home. It was not just in Italy; I also found exceptionally good fruit in France. I was intrigued by flat Saturn peaches that I had not seen before. I sat in the street and ate three of them immediately after purchase, juice dripping down my fingers.

The walk was generally quite easy today. There was a nice section of a few kilometres along the river before entering Lucca that was very enjoyable, with shade and seats. But the final stretch through the suburbs of Lucca was on very hot streets.

I had an excellent lunch—in fact, two back-to-back lunches—at the main piazza in front of Lucca Cathedral, among throngs of tourists. My neighbours surreptitiously watched me as I wolfed down my food with my pack and various bits of equipment spread out around me. I certainly did not fit the mould of typical tourists thronging Lucca.

The city with its well-preserved wall is wonderful. No wonder that Lucca is a very popular tourist destination. But crowds of tourists really put me off, after having spent so long walking through quiet countryside and small towns.

My hotel was okay, but I felt there was nothing special to keep me in Lucca tomorrow. I decided to skip the rest day and continue to Altopascio.

I felt very tired and worn out today. My companions had scattered to the winds, and I was feeling lonely again.

Lucca to Altopascio (3 July)

I did not wake fully refreshed and the pack felt like a lead weight dragging me down all day. I became unwell as the day progressed and each slow step was something of a struggle. One misses the support of companions at such times. The route was often along roads and was quite unpleasant at times. Heat rose from the tarmac and drove up through my feet. I became very footsore. I think it got to 35 degrees Celsius today, but considerably hotter on the baking road.

Some of the off-road paths had been greatly improved for pilgrims. Such improvements seem to depend very much on the initiative of local pilgrim associations and the availability of funding. The Via Francigena is a European cultural project, so I hope those bureaucrats in Brussels occasionally toss a few crumbs to fund improvement projects.

I perked up a bit after a long rest in the Ostello per Pellegrini and a meal in the cool of the evening. Hopefully I will recover enough overnight to continue to San Miniato tomorrow. Another pilgrim arrived and bustled about doing her chores while I rested in my room.

The famous pilgrim hospital at Altopascio was run by the Knights of Tau, who also founded daughter houses in other parts of Europe. The Knights chose the Greek letter *tau* for their symbol for various reasons, including its resemblance to the Christian Cross. I would encounter the tau cross again.

The hospital eventually fell into decline and some of the buildings became part of a large farm. The dominating Romanesque bell tower and other remnants of the original complex still survive. The bell tower houses 'La Smarrita' ('the lost one'), which was sounded at dusk to guide pilgrims to safety after crossing a difficult stretch of marshlands on the ancient Via Francigena. La Smarrita is still sounded every July 25 on the feast of St. Jacob, when there is a town procession evoking the past of the Knights of Tau.

Altopascio to San Miniato (4 July)

I set out at 6:30 am, still a little tired, but mostly recovered. I walked on the main road on several occasions to avoid detours into the fields. The road was busy in both directions and quite dangerous in places (no verge, blind corners). It would be best avoided in poor visibility or rain.

A short distance outside Altopascio the route continues to Galleno along remnants of the ancient Via Francigena, with traces of paving thought to date from medieval times. Little remains except some large, uneven paving. These large stones were originally covered with smaller stones and pebbles to make the going easier. As the route fell into disuse, the top covering would have been washed away to expose the foundation. Cycles of wet and dry, freezing and thawing would then have created the very uneven surface that now exists.

Remnants of ancient roads, an old boundary stone, a stream crossing and the old Greppi hostel made this one of the more evocative sections on the Via Francigena. There were a number of explanatory signs in Italian and English that further enhanced the feeling of being connected with those long-ago days. It was quite simple, but well done.

On arrival at the Convento San Francesco in San Miniato, pilgrims are given a small wooden "Tau" pendant to hang around their neck. The accommodation is in separate rooms, both singles and doubles. One wall of the hall is entirely decorated, from floor to ceiling, with astonishing, Picasso-esque murals. I wish I knew the story behind that explosion of exuberant art.

Another pilgrim was staying here and we had a very enjoyable dinner with the Franciscan brothers after Mass: soup, pasta, salad, fish, fruit and drinks. Staying in religious houses like this was a special highlight of the Via Francigena in Italy. The atmosphere was calm and reflective—and very healing at day's end.

San Miniato to Gambassi Terme (Sigeric stop XX) (5 July)

I had the most wonderful, deep sleep and woke refreshed and ready to go after an excellent breakfast with the Franciscan Brothers and a new walking companion. She was the lady whom I met yesterday at Altopascio, who had become badly lost and wanted to walk with me to avoid a repeat. She would be walking with me to Siena.

The off-road paths were gradually changing to brown, dusty soil; along the ridges of rolling Tuscan hills with vineyards and olive groves, and the pencil pine trees so evocative of the region.

We met an elderly Italian couple, sitting in their garden in a small village, who offered us water when we stopped for a break. Having someone with me who was Italian dissolved the barriers that can separate foreign pilgrims from local people and we had a more comfortable and relaxed conversation as a result. Such connections were very precious to me, when strangers were able to erase the barriers that seemed to separate them. Strangers are more than just stereotypes to be shunned, or even feared. We all share the same human longings and the same sufferings; we are all grateful for kindness.

Our accommodation at the Ostello Sigerico was another highlight of the Via Francigena. It is in a very tranquil setting with panoramic views of Gambasi Terme and the countryside. I sat in the garden in the golden summer light before sunset and admired the view. The *Ostello* is part of the restored buildings, but you can still relate the to the ancient church complex to the modern construction. The old church was very interesting and the *Ostello* owner gave us a short tour.

The *Ostello* is a little distance from the town centre and we had a stiff climb to get there to enjoy a late afternoon coffee and stroll in the gardens.

Another pilgrim arrived about 9 pm as we were finishing dinner. He had walked 52 kilometres that day and seemed hell-bent on reaching Rome in record time. Why all the hurry? We are driven and pressured so much in our daily lives that it is good to take time out to enjoy a slower and more reflective pace.

Gambassi Terme to San Gimignano (Sigeric stop XIX) (6 July)

The number of walkers and cyclists had increased quite a bit now that we were in the heart of Tuscan tourist country. We met two Spanish pilgrims with guitars who were walking home to Santiago. Another young man was walking home to Martigny after serving two years in the Vatican's Swiss Guards. Cyclists with heavy panniers often passed us.

The walk was very enjoyable, across rolling Tuscan hills, with vineyards and olive groves. We had a brief stop at the beautiful, tranquil Monastero di Bose. This vibrant monastic community has over eighty brothers and sisters from different Christian backgrounds. The Monastero attracts thousands of visitors each year.

Then we had our first glimpses of the famous towers of San Gimignano on a hilltop, hazy at first in the shimmering summer heat. We arrived early in the afternoon and had lunch in the piazza; *bruschetta e pomodoro* and an excellent Tuscan soup, full of bread, a meal in itself. The rest of today was spent settling into our rooms at the Monastero di San Girolamo and hanging out in the crowded piazzas of San Gimignano.

San Gimignano to Monteriggione (7 July)

We took the alternate route via Colle di Val d'Elsa. The village is somewhat reminiscent of San Gimignano without the tourists. The lack of distractions and the quietness made it very appealing to me. Colle di Val d'Elsa has been renowned for the production of crystal glassware and art since the 17th century. It produces about 15 percent of the world's crystal.

The approach to Monteriggione was very impressive, with the castle walls and its towers dominating the hilltop, looming ever closer. It is one of the most important walled castles in the province according to its own publicity blurb. The area inside the walls has become the central square with cafes, bars and shops. You can climb up and walk along part of the walls (free entrance if you show your pilgrim passport), with good views over the town and countryside.

Monteriggione was a great place to spend a night. We stayed at the Casa per Ferie Santa Maria Assunta Ospitalita Pellegrini, right on the main square, and ate dinner al fresco on the piazza with another remarkable pilgrim. She had just returned from Afghanistan on an International Mission to train local police men and women; and was walking the Via Francigena after an eventful year that included a suicide bombing of the base where she was stationed.

Monteriggione to Siena (Sigeric stop XV) (8 July)

The first part of the walk to Siena was on pleasant forest tracks and paths. Forests can present navigational challenges, because the paths often change and new paths appear. As the designated navigator I felt a particular responsibility to take care of my companion and not get us lost. There were quite a few ups and downs today, with a final uphill slog to Siena.

Of the three major tourist attractions on this section of the Via Francigena–Lucca, San Gimignano and Siena–Siena is the most spectacular in terms of its buildings and cultural heritage. We had lunch with the staff at the Accoglienza Santa Luisa, where we also spent the night. Some were religious, but others were lay people. All were very friendly, laughing and having a good time together during our communal meal. There was a relaxed family atmosphere and the strong bonds between them all were obvious.

We wandered about for the afternoon admiring the sights, especially the breathtaking Duomo. But everyone gravitates back to the Campo. It seemed too small for a horse race (the turns would be very tight) and it is on a slight slope. The Palio must be quite dangerous for horses and riders, even though the paving is covered with sand for the event.

According to one shopkeeper, Sienese are always talking about the Palio; the one just finished, and when that topic has been done to death, the next Palio. "It is so boring!" she exclaimed, then confessed that she was born in a different city and only moved to Siena recently. Soon she will be singing the praises of the Palio like everyone else.

Tomorrow my companion of the last few days will set off for home and I will trudge on alone towards Rome. It is a depressing prospect.

Siena to Ponte d'Arbia (Sigeric stop XIV) (9 July)

My companion woke early so we could say goodbye. I had an easy walk today, with a big descent out of Siena then rather flat and open all the way to Ponte d'Arbia. But I desperately missed the company of my companion and felt very down.

The accommodation (Centro Cresti) was quite good, but the town itself had little to offer. The pizzeria across the road was closed for summer, and the small supermarket was also closed. There was a good bar where I bought snacks and some basic foods for my dinner.

Ponte d'Arbia to San Quirico d'Orcia
(Sigeric stop XII) (10 July)

There was a thunderstorm with torrential rain shortly before dawn. How wonderful it was to snuggle in a dry bed, sheltered from the raging elements, lulled by the sound of rain on the roof.

The storm soon passed and I set out after breakfast in cool weather with beautiful, soft light defining the trees and fields. Alas, the pleasant stroll soon became a muddy, slippery slog on uneven, rutted farm tracks soaked by the rain. Clods of heavy clay built up on my boots and the going was slow as I stumbled about.

Black clouds gathered ahead of me in the afternoon, with rumbles of distant thunder, getting ever closer. There was no danger yet, but I was conscious of being in the open and exposed to lightning. Fortunately I did not have a walking pole pointed to the sky like a personal lightning rod.

The skies opened with a torrent of rain just as I reached shelter in San Quirico. There was a brief scattering of small hail stones towards the end of the storm, bouncing off the paving in the piazza. Then the rain died away, the sky cleared, the sun appeared and it became quite cool. How exciting it was to experience raw displays of nature from the comfort of shelter!

I met the pilgrim who had returned from Afghanistan, and we wandered about the town—it was quite pretty and interesting—and had coffee until the Collegiata dei Santi Quirico e Giulitta opened to let pilgrims in for the night. Several of us had settled into the ground floor dormitory, when we were mysteriously moved to another dormitory on the second floor.

San Quirico d'Orcia to Radicofani (11 July)

The day started cold and clear but became hot later on. Much of the route was along ridges between lines of bare, rolling hills, with great views. The last section before Radicofani was relentlessly uphill with a steepish gradient that was quite tiring at the end of a long, hot day. It was made a little easier by being on a road where I could establish a regular rhythm.

I received a wonderful welcome at the accommodation run by two members of the Confraternita di San Jacopo di Compostella. Cold drinks and slices of fruit were pressed on me. There were five of us staying here, including my new companion from yesterday; and a friend of the owner and his wife, who had walked with them to Jerusalem and written a book about it.

That got my attention. I had been idly wondering what I would do after I had completed the Via Francigena and I had been thinking of continuing to Jerusalem next year. Some years ago in France I met a retired French man who had started walking in Jerusalem and was on his way to Santiago, Spain. It was before the present Syrian conflict and he had been able to travel overland to Greece and then take a ship to Italy to continue walking along the Via Francigena until he would have to branch off onto the pilgrimage route to Santiago. I had never heard of anyone undertaking such an incredible journey. I have since learned that a number of people do variants of the trip each year. But all that is for the future.

Radicofani is very attractive, as are all the small hilltop towns in this part of Italy, with their jumbled buildings, and tiny piazzas which surprise you as you unexpectedly stumble into them. The town is dominated by a castle dating from 978 AD. There is a nice park with great views over the countryside.

Before dinner we sat down on a bench in our bare feet. Our hostess, dressed in a special costume, knelt before us and, one by one, gently washed our feet, dried them and gave each foot a brief kiss. Our host, in a similar costume, said a short prayer; with each of us joining in the Responses as our own feet were washed.

It was a memorable experience that bonded us together in a way that is difficult to describe. Two young Italian sisters, so close it seemed they could read each other's thoughts; a German policewoman just back from the dangers of a year in Afghanistan and readjusting to an ordinary life back in Europe; the pilgrim who had walked to Jerusalem and who spoke of the emotional power of walking through the Holy Land; and me, a restless seeker from a far country who found support and inspiration in their company. We were truly blessed to share in such an experience.

We then moved to the long dining table to enjoy a very pleasant and filling dinner in each other's company, the owners caring for us all. A dinner that was mentally as well as physically restorative.

As I thought back over my time walking the Via Francigena, from the first day I set out from Canterbury, I have been privileged to have met and stayed with some special people–such as those here at Radicofani. I admire and respect them all so much.

Radicofani to Aquapendente (Sigeric stop IX) (12 July)

All of us were early starters and we had an excellent breakfast together before parting company. We each preferred to walk alone, but would meet each other again at the end of the day. Our hostess waited at the door of the Casa in her cloak and gave each of us a blessing, and a prayer for our journey.

I followed the official route to Ponte a Rigo, then diverted to the "new" official route beside the main road. It was generally on safe tracks parallel to the road, but there were stretches on the road itself. The verges were good so the road was reasonably safe. The official route in my guidebook took a big detour into the fields, so I saved several kilometres today. The walking was easy. First I had a long descent in fog and then it was flat all the way to Aquapendente, finishing with the usual uphill slog into the town centre.

The early part of the walk was on the old Via Cassia, with long stretches of ancient cobbles, and the ruins of an ancient building still visible. The Via Cassia was an important Roman road which started in Rome and passed through several towns along the Via

Francigena. In fact, pilgrims walk along the busy modern Via Cassia on the final stage into Rome.

Aquapendente was an important staging post on the pilgrimage route to Rome and the Holy Land. The Monastery was directly subordinate to the Holy Sepulchre at Jerusalem and a Templar house was annexed to it. I stayed at the Convento Cappuccini, Casa San Lazzaro, in a quiet location at the top of a stiff climb.

It was full of American and Italian high school students on summer camp, helping at an archaeological dig in the area. They had the day off and were enjoying a huge communal lunch in the garden, under shady trees and a trellis of vines when I arrived. As I ate my lunch in the kitchen, several of the Americans dropped in to offer me food or any help I might need. They had obviously been well-nagged by parents and teachers at home to be polite to others while they were in Italy.

Then I sat under shady trees in the garden, writing and admiring the well-tended vegetable patch; wondering if foraging among the tempting produce would be OK, but I decided against it. The garden had to provide food for all those ravenous students. The students finished their lunch and were having a great time tossing a ball around and teasing each other. Not a computer or smartphone to be seen! Yes, it's true! They were bursting with energy and the carefree innocence of youth that the responsibilities of adult life would eventually beat out of them. Thankfully it won't work in all cases and a few mavericks and adventurers will survive unbeaten to explore and discover.

Suddenly it dawned on me that in another week I would be in Rome. What a shock! I immediately dismissed the thought. "It ain't over till it's over" as the American baseballer Yogi Berra wisely said.

Tomorrow I will walk to Bolsena and its beautiful lake. How I long to see it after the disappointment of the sea near Massa.

Aquapendente to Bolsena (Sigeric stop VIII) (13 July)

It rained in the night, but I set out under clearing skies and in cool weather, excited by the prospect of seeing Lake Bolsena.

Strange crops: An array of solar panels was set amid fields of crops, buzzing in the early light as they woke and started to track the energising sun, like robotic sunflowers. Then I passed a field of real sunflowers, quietly soaking up the goodness of soil and sun. There was also corn, not yet "as high as an elephant's eye".

I had coffee at San Lorenzo, in a bustling café with people coming and going, calling out Sunday greetings, air-kissing each other on each cheek. One of the great things about walking in Italy was being able to merge into the crowd at bars and cafés. Sometimes curious locals would ask about my journey, and they would always offer help if needed. Once I was asked to write a greeting and sign a local travel brochure as a memento of my visit. A sense of community was often apparent in small Italian towns, where the people loved to get together at cafés and gossip–or just enjoy each other's company for a few moments.

San Lorenzo was a very nice, busy town with a holiday atmosphere, probably because it was near Lake Bolsena and full of weekend holiday makers. One of my companions stayed here last night rather than at the Convento in Aquapendente. She said it was an excellent place for a night and I tend to agree. Aquapendente was not particularly interesting for me, but I did not have the time or inclination to explore its cultural and historical places of interest.

Shortly after leaving San Lorenzo I had my first view of Lake Bolsena, a vast expanse of silver, shimmering water. My heart almost burst with pleasure at the sight of such a noble lake nestling in the embrace of soft, round hills.

The rest of the walk to Bolsena was on quiet roads among farms and trees, with tantalising glimpses of the lake. It was extremely pretty, another of my memorable walks along the Via Francigena. This is a volcanic region. Lakes Bolsena and Vico are essentially the collapsed craters of large, extinct volcanos. The last major eruptions were in Roman times, but their evidence was all around me. I passed a quarry of red volcanic gravel. The dirt paths were mostly red from the same material.

Bolsena is a very attractive town. It is a place of saints and miracles that are explained in the Church of Santa Cristina on the main piazza. As a result, the Church became a place of pilgrimage. The old town and castle overlooking the area is also very atmospheric, with narrow stone streets, lots of bars and shops, and great views, thronged with holiday makers.

The lake shore was some distance from the town centre, perhaps a kilometre, with tree-lined streets full of cafés and souvenir shops. People were having fun on pebbly beaches. It reminded me a little of the walk along Lake Geneva that I keep harping on about.

I stayed at the Instituto Suore Ss. Sacramento with its welcoming Sisters. There were four pilgrims staying here, including three I had already met.

Bolsena to Montefiascone (Sigeric stop VII) (14 July)

Much of the early part of the walk was through attractive forest, with an unseen stream tinkling over rocks somewhere among the trees. Elsewhere the grapes were getting bigger in neat vineyards as summer advanced.

I arrived early at the attractive town of Montefiascone and had coffee while trying to decide my route for the next few days. The pilgrim back from Afghanistan turned up and we had coffee together. She spoke so glowingly of the Monastero di San Pietro here that I decided to stay there with her and call it a rest day. It was also raining lightly, so I needed little convincing. We received a very welcoming reception at the Monastero. The Sister who looked after us was in a jovial mood and made light-hearted comments as she showed us to our rooms that stretched my Italian to its limits.

Montefiascone has some interesting places to see, notably the Cathedral and its impressive dome. I read somewhere that the dome is the largest in Italy after St. Peter's in Rome.

I dined that night on soup, pasta, vegetables, potato omelette, cherries, and wine if desired. It was definitely one of my better meals of the last few weeks. Of course, the surroundings and people add to the enjoyment of any meal, not to mention ravenous hunger.

Montefiascone to San Martino al Cimino (15 July)

There was a choice of two quite different routes for the next few days. The official route is via Viterbo, Vetralla (Sigeric stop V), Campranica and Sutri; over essentially flat terrain. I took another route which climbs through forest, with some steep gradients, to Lake Vico, before descending to the official route again. The main incentive for me was to see the lake. There was a relaxing descent to Viterbo (Sigeric stop VI) through open farmland, walking on sections of the ancient paved road.

In Medieval times gallows were sometimes erected in the area, in view of passing travellers, as a warning to thieves preying on pilgrims. I thought later that this custom should be revived on St. Peter's Square in Rome as a warning to street stalls selling over-priced drinks and ice cream.

Viterbo's historic centre is one of the best preserved medieval towns of central Italy, but I did not have time to explore it properly as I walked through. Leaving the town, I walked to San Martino, mostly in forest and often on narrow, steep tracks. But they were well-walked and fairly clear.

There was a very helpful café (Pizzamania) just opposite the arched entry to the Abbey complex, where I had a meal and asked about accommodation. The staff checked out a couple of places and showed me the way on Google Maps, even offering to drive me.

The town itself was not particularly interesting to me, apart from the Abbey of San Martino. It is a large monastery that serves as the mother house of the Cistercian Order in Italy.

San Martino al Cimino to Sutri (Sigeric stop III) (16 July)

The day was already warm when I started the long, slow climb through forests to Lake Vico. It was difficult to believe that it was once a huge volcano. The path followed the lake for some distance, but no closer than about 500 metres. I caught only occasional, tantalising glimpses of the water through the trees, shining brightly in the reflected light of early morning; with no wind to ruffle the surface. One or two paths branched off the Via Francigena and seemed to lead down to a road circling the Lake, but I did not have time to explore the possibility of getting down to the shore.

After passing the lake, the route from Campranica to Sutri was mainly through forest, with rustic bridges periodically crossing and recrossing a small stream, and a picnic table that made a tranquil place for a break.

The Monastero Santissima Concezione in Sutri was full when a Japanese girl and I tried to get a room, but they gave us a list of other places to stay and we went to the Hotel Sutrium. She started walking in Turkey and was heading for Santiago in Spain. She had walked many pilgrimage routes, including the 88 Temple Pilgrimage, Japan's most famous pilgrimage route, a 1200 kilometre loop around the island of Shikoku. She wants to cycle from Japan across Asia to Turkey, "to link my home to Santiago," she said. Why not?

People might pour cold water on her dream and tell her it would be too difficult, or unsafe, or unfitting for a Japanese woman. Cold water and dreams go together. Life beats the dreams out of so many people, their yearnings unfulfilled and hidden in their hearts with all the other "might-have-beens" of their lives. But a seed can sprout after many years of lying dormant, waiting for the right conditions to burst forth into a plant that may bear a beautiful flower. *Die Blaue Blume*. Dreams can too–when our lives are, once more, ready for them. So, in a quiet receptive moment, by the shores of a dreaming lake with soft water lapping on the sand, or among

81

flowery uplands where the sky seems within our reach; when our hearts are open and we are free, let us peer deep inside ourselves. Perhaps a long-forgotten seed is stirring into life.

Three more days to go!

Sutri to Compagnano di Roma (17 July)

The route passes an Etruscan necropolis on the outskirts of Sutri, with numerous tombs cut into the rock. Sutri was a strategic town on the Via Cassia in Roman times, but it had been an Etruscan town in pre-Christian times. The tomb contents have long since disappeared or been looted, and the caves themselves have been used for storage or for sheltering animals.

I took the road route to avoid another detour into fields. The day was very hot and I longed for cool drinks; but Monterosi was the only town with bars where I could quench my thirst with something other than plain water. After Monterosi much of the route was without shelter until the last few kilometres into Compagnano di Roma, where it was under trees. While resting in the shade, I met a cyclist who gave me a shot of very strong coffee from his thermos flask; which energised me for the steep climb up to the town.

I had a snack in an excellent café on the central square and decided to ask about a place to stay for the night. I composed an enquiry in my mind and turned to the man seated at the next table.

"Mi scusi. Dove si trova l'Oratorio San Giovanni, per favore?"

"Pardon? I am American," he replied. "On vacation."

An efficient young Italian woman nearby overheard the exchange and immediately took charge, firing up Google Maps on her laptop and busily researching options for me. A couple of young men from other tables joined in, rather unnecessarily I thought, (but she was very pretty) and I was soon on my way, instructions ringing in my ears.

The accommodation at Oratorio San Giovanni Battista was very basic, with mattresses on the floor and in need of sweeping (which I did), but it was okay for one night. The priest who led me to the dormitory was very jovial, so that was nice.

A cool change arrived late in the afternoon bringing cloud and distant thunder, an invigorating end to a hot day.

I enjoyed a filling pilgrim dinner at a bar next to the Oratorio with two other pilgrims—pasta, steak with salad, water. A good meal once again made all well with the world.

Compagnano di Roma to La Storta (Sigeric stop II) (18 July)

There was an interesting river crossing today. The path was quite steep on both sides of the stream and would be slippery in wet weather. Fortunately, at this time of year the water was low enough to expose the stepping stones and I had no problems crossing. But I tested each stepping stone to make sure it was firmly in place and able to take my weight.

Earlier, I had met an older pilgrim resting against a shady embankment on the path, with his boots off and his backpack beside him, looking very tired and lethargic. I stopped for a chat. "I have only walked a short way, but I am feeling very tired," he confessed. He made no sign of wanting to join me, so at length I continued my journey. But I was concerned afterwards about how he would negotiate the tricky river crossing. He seemed alert and well when I left him, so I hoped he was alright.

I stayed at the Instituto Figlie di Nostra Signora dei Sacro Cuore in La Storta. Check-in was almost like at a hotel. In fact the brochure in my room advertised it as a convenient "hotel" for visitors to Rome wanting to avoid the crowds in the city itself. There are good train connections to the city, so it was not a crazy idea.

I asked if I could attend Vespers at 7 pm and the head Sister said it would be OK. The Chapel was full with about 25 Sisters when I walked in and took my place at the back of the Chapel. This occasioned some stirring and quick glances among the Sisters, and I was a little uneasy that I might be disturbing them. But I was completely forgotten in the harmony and spirituality of the Service, enveloped in the beautiful, ethereal singing of the Sisters.

After Vespers we all moved into the dining room for dinner. I was placed at a separate table well apart from the Sisters. There were no other pilgrims staying here. The Sisters were relaxed and animated among themselves, ignoring me completely. I felt relieved I was not intruding on them. The cook brought in our meals and joked with everyone as he handed round the plates. I can't remember all the dishes. It was Friday, so one must have been fish. We finished with ice cream. I went to bed stuffed to the gills. There was a Rule of Silence in the evenings from 9 pm.

It was an excellent place for me to take time out to reflect on the Via Francigena, to relax in comfortable, tranquil surroundings, to stroll in the small olive grove and prepare for the final stage to St. Peter's tomorrow.

There was happiness mixed with sadness at the prospect of Journey's End. Canterbury, where I started out on the Via Francigena three years ago, was far in the past now. Memories from that long journey rose before me; the aching beauty of lakes and mountains and of all the creatures that inhabit our Earth. But especially memories of people who had shared the walk with me, who I admire immensely; and people who were kind to me as I passed briefly through their lives. They will always remain an inspiration to me, shining brightly in my heart, giving me strength to go on when the way ahead is difficult.

"Through many dangers, toils and snares
I have already come;
'Tis Grace that brought me safe thus far
and Grace will lead me home."
(Amazing Grace).

La Storta to St. Peter's Square (19 July)

Most of the route today was on busy, unpleasant city roads. I could understand why some pilgrims choose to take the train into the city for this final stage. There is a short alternate path (about 5 kilometres) through a nature reserve that avoids some of the roads; but it was overgrown with brambles and impassable when I tried it, and I had to retrace my steps back to the road.

There were also a few kilometres of the Via Francigena through parkland just before entering the city streets of Rome, with benches where you can sit to admire the first panoramic views of Rome and the distant dome of St. Peter's Basilica. Then there was a steep descent to the city streets on a horrible, roughly-cobbled path that zig-zagged steeply downhill.

I made my way through throngs of tourists heading for St. Peter's Square, along streets lined with souvenir shops and drink stalls. I wanted to buy a large badge or pendant with St. Peter's crossed keys to attach to my pack. But I saw only small badges you can pin to your hat or shirt.

The Via Francigena enters the Square with the Basilica and its dome on the right. Tourists were lined up all the way to the security screening station in front of the Basilica. Crowds were milling about, taking photos, admiring the sights, talking. I walked across the Square to get my *Testimonium* as having completed the Via Francigena. The brief formalities were completed in an ordinary information office with no special ceremony, only the crossed keys of St. Peter above the door to mark the place.

I managed to have a farewell dinner with one of my companions who had crossed the Po River with me in Danilo's boat, and with whom I exchanged frequent text messages over the following weeks. The pilgrim back from Afghanistan had taken a different route and I never saw her again, which was a great disappointment for me. All the others who had briefly passed in and out of my life had scattered to the four winds and our lives have diverged. In spite of all these partings, we will forever share a special bond: for a brief time we were together on one of the greatest of all pilgrimages, the Via Francigena, a journey of over 2000 kilometres.

Rome (Sigeric stop I) (20 July)

The Pope was giving his Sunday address in St. Peter's Square today, so I put off visiting the seven Pilgrim Churches until tomorrow. A rest day at last! Writing postcards, hanging about St. Peter's Square. No pack! Wearing comfortable sandals! The simplest things become the most indulgent luxuries after a long walk.

St. Peter's Square filled rapidly with excited people as noon approached. Tourists were milling about. Sisters waited singly, or clustered in small groups while they waited for the important moment. A couple of robed Brothers strode busily through the crowd on some errand or other. Groups from other countries were having a great time, waving banners and flags, singing and chanting "Viva Papa!"

Two big TV screens were set up to televise the speech so that everyone could get a good view. The crowd went wild when the Pope appeared in the window and began to speak, clapping enthusiastically throughout when he said something particularly pleasing. He finished by wishing us a good lunch, and the crowd dispersed, slowly and a little reluctantly. People stood around, taking photos of their groups, hugging, chatting to others. Pilgrims from other countries waved flags. It was wonderful.

Rome (21 July)

Sigeric spent only two days in Rome but visited 23 churches. My task to visit only the seven pilgrim churches seemed much easier. But they opened about 9:30 am, closed about noon and re-opened again at about 4:30 pm. So I had to plan the day carefully. The metro made it easy to get around, but there was still considerable walking involved. It would be a very full day to see all seven churches.

There is a dress code for inside the churches. Knee-length shorts are okay but nothing shorter. Enterprising street sellers were selling women a length of light fabric they could wrap around their waist like a skirt to satisfy the dress code. I was able to get a pilgrim stamp for my pilgrim passport by asking at the Sacristy in each church.

The Basilica of St. Paul Outside-the-Walls was the most moving for me. It is set in beautiful, park-like surroundings, with very few tourists, just visitors relaxing or snacking on the grass. Inside, they were quiet and respectful, unlike at many of the other churches. There is a lovely internal courtyard garden here, overlooked by an impressive decoration on the pediment of the Basilica roof (the triangular end of the roof). You can buy food and eat in the garden if you choose.

I walked down some steps to kneel at the tomb of St. Paul. There is a chain above the tomb which is reputed to be the one that bound him as a prisoner in Rome. A family with two young children came down after I had stepped away and knelt quietly for a few moments of family reflection. It was a very intimate experience.

This church was a far more fitting and peaceful place to end my pilgrimage than the busy, crowded St. Peter's Square.

o o o

Photographs

Photo 1: A statue of St. Peter, carrying his trademark key in his right hand. The statue is on the Ponte St. Pietro over the Serchio River just before Lucca.

Photos 2 and 3: Enthusiastic pilgrims in St. Peter's Square, after the Pope's Sunday speech.

Epilogue

Weeks later, as I sat at home going over the long journey again in my mind, reviewing the notes and photos I had taken over three years, it had taken on a dreamlike quality.

Memories change and fade, but some remain forever, shining bright. Such memories can guide us to more fulfilled lives, like beacons in a dark, storm-wracked sea guiding weary mariners to a safe haven.

There is a universal human need for pilgrimage, not only for the joy of accomplishing a difficult task, but also because it can be a search for something that will give us comfort for the hurts and pains of our lives, and hope for the future.

When I walked the Camino Frances to Santiago, I met a woman who was undertaking the pilgrimage as a way of giving thanks for the blessings she had received in her life: a good partner, fine children and the material comforts of a successful career. They are things we often take for granted.

Whatever their reasons for setting out, there is nobility in overcoming doubt and the hardships of body and mind that all pilgrims must face on their journeys.

The spirits of all those other pilgrims who have travelled the Via Francigena since ancient days were always with me, and I drew on their strength when the journey seemed to be too hard to bear, as I walked my personal Via Francigena, one day at a time.

Some years ago I trekked to Gokyo Ri, a mountain in Nepal not far from Everest Base Camp. It took eight arduous days to reach the high camp by a glacial lake at the base of the final peak.

I met a lady who had already made the long trek, but who had failed in her first attempt to reach the summit of the mountain. But on this day she succeeded, breathing with difficulty in the thin air almost 5500 metres above sea level.

In the distance Mt Everest, Chomolungma, the holy mountain, shone dazzling white. Wisps of snow streamed fiercely from the summit in the jetstream often present at that altitude. All around us were vast, craggy mountains, cloaked in gleaming white snow and bluish ice, jostled together in the greatest mountain range on earth. Prayer flags fluttered in the wind, carrying their messages into the great unknown.

Far below I saw the milky blue lake from which we began our ascent, with our tiny tents nestled on its shore. A jagged glacier wound down the valley, an icy dragon slowly edging its way to a distant river, there to melt into waters feeding Mother Ganges, and, at last, to disappear into the immense ocean that girdles our planet.

Next year the monsoons will come again to carry those waters deep into the mountains, feeding the snow and glaciers and completing another great, endless cycle of renewal—a cycle that lies at the heart of the Buddhist faith.

I greatly admired that lady who had struggled to succeed in her climb, and who now stood with me on a lofty mountain so far from home, just as I will always admire all those unsung pilgrims who have overcome much to undertake their great journeys.

May you—and people of all faiths—find fulfilment, comfort and hope on the Via Francigena, the Way of St. James or on a holy mountain—or on some other personal journey that can only be measured deep within our being.

The value of such a journey is not defined by the distance travelled, or by the opinions of other people; it is defined by ourselves alone for the personal blessings it has inscribed in our hearts, in our minds and on our bodies.

Afterword

I hope more people will travel the Via Francigena after reading my book. Not everyone has the time or inclination to walk it all at once. Let that not be a barrier. It took me three years. But for people who don't want to complete the whole walk, there are special sections that can be done in one or two weeks; such as the evocative World War One battlefields in France, and the beautiful countryside from Lausanne to the St. Bernard Pass in Switzerland. Italy also offers many wonderful sections that can be walked in a few days or a week.

Many early pilgrims continued on to Jerusalem. I am tempted to do the same next year, encouraged by the people I met at Radicofani. My only fear is that my pilgrimage obsession is getting out of control, and that after Jerusalem I will meet someone who tells me about yet another wonderful pilgrimage. Just like the shop owner at St. Jean Pied de Port who first made me aware of the Via Francigena in 2010.

List of Stages

Via Francigena—2012

Canterbury to Colred (July 19)

Colred to Calais (July 20)

Calais to Guînes (July 22)

Guînes to Licques (July 23)

Licques to Wisques (July 24)

Wisques to Therouanne (25 July)

Therouanne to Amettes (26 July)

Amettes to Bruay la Buissière (Sigeric stop LXXVI) (27 July)

Bruay la Buissière to Arras (Sigeric stop LXXV)(28 July)

Arras to Bapaume (30 July)

Bapaume to Peronne (31 July)

Peronne to Trefcon (1 August)

Trefcon to Seraucourt le Grand (Sigeric stop LXXIII) (2 August)

Seraucourt le Grand to Laon (Sigeric stop LXXII) (3 August)

Laon to Reims (Sigeric stop LXX) (4 August)

Reims to Trepail (6 August)

Trepail to Châlons en Champagne (Sigeric stop LXIX) (7 August)

Châlons en Champagne to Coole (8 August)

Coole to le Meix-Tiercelin (9 August)

Le Meix-Tiercelin to Brienne le Château (10 August)

Brienne le Château to Bar sur Aube (Sigeric stop LXV) (11 August)

Bar sur Aube to Clairvaux sur Aube (12 August)

Clairvaux sur Aube to Châteauvillain (14 August)

Châteauvillain to Villers sur Suize (15 August)

Villers sur Suize to Langres (16 August)

Langres to les Archots (18 August)

les Archots to Champlitte (19 August)

Champlitte to Dampierre sur Salon (20 August)

Dampierre sur Salon to Gy (21 August)

Gy to Geneuille (22 August)

Geneuille to Besançon (Sigeric stop LIX) (23 August)

Via Francigena—2013

Besançon (June 17)

Besançon to Trépot (June 18)

Trépot to Aubonne (June 19)

Aubonne to Pontarlier (Sigeric stop LVII) (20 June)

Pontarlier to Jougne (21 June)

Jougne to Orbe (22 June)

Orbe to Echallens (23 June)

Echallens to Cully (24 June)

Cully to Villeneuve (25 June)

Villeneuve to St. Maurice (Sigeric stop LI) (26 June)

St. Maurice to Martigny (27 June)

Martigny to Orsières (Sigeric stop L) (28 June)

Orsières to Bourg St. Pierre (Sigeric stop XLIX) (29 June)

Bourg St. Pierre to Col Grand St. Bernard (30 June)

Col Grand St. Bernard to Etroubles (1 July)

Etroubles to Aosta (Sigeric stop XLVII) (2 July)

Aosta (3 July)

Aosta to Chatillon (4 July)

Chatillon to Verres (5 July)

Verres to Pont Saint Martin (6 July)

Pont Saint Martin to Ivrea (Sigeric stop XLV) (7 July)

Ivrea to Roppolo (8 July)

Roppolo to San Germano (9 July)

San Germano to Vercelli (Sigeric stop XLIII) (10 July)

Via Francigena—2014

Vercelli to Robbio (15 June)

Robbio to Mortara (16 June)

Mortara to Bozzolo (17 June)

Bozzolo to Pavia (Sigeric stop XLI) (18 June)

Pavia to Santa Cristina (Sigeric stop XL) (19 June)

Santa Cristina to Orio Litta (20 June)

Orio Litta to Crossing the Po River to Piacenza (Sigeric stop XXXVIII) (21 June)

Piacenza to Fiorenzuola d'Arda (Sigeric stop XXXVII) (22 June)

Fiorenzuola d'Arda to Fidenza (Sigeric stop XXXVI) (23 June)

Fidenza to Medesano (Sigeric stop XXXV) (24 June)

Medesano to Cassio (25 June)

Cassio to Ostello della Cisa (26 June)

Ostello della Cisa to Pontremoli (Sigeric stop XXXI) (27 June)

Pontremoli to Aulla (Sigeric stop XXX) (28 June)

Aulla to Sarzana (29 June)

Sarzana to Massa (30 June)

Massa to Camaiore (Sigeric stop XXVII) (1 July)

Camaiore to Lucca (Sigeric stop XXVI) (2 July)

Lucca to Altopascio (3 July)

Altopascio to San Miniato (4 July)

San Miniato to Gambassi Terme (Sigeric stop XX) (5 July)

Gambassi Terme to San Gimignano (Sigeric stop XIX) (6 July)

San Gimignano to Monteriggione (7 July)

Monteriggione to Siena (8 July)

Siena to Ponte d'Arbia (Sigeric stop XIV) (9 July)

Printed in Great Britain
by Amazon.co.uk, Ltd.,
Marston Gate.